BLUE MIRACLE

NEW YORK GIANTS 2008 SUPER BOWL CHAMPIONS

DAILY NEWS

SP
SPORTS
PUBLISHING
L.L.C.

SportsPublishingLLC.com

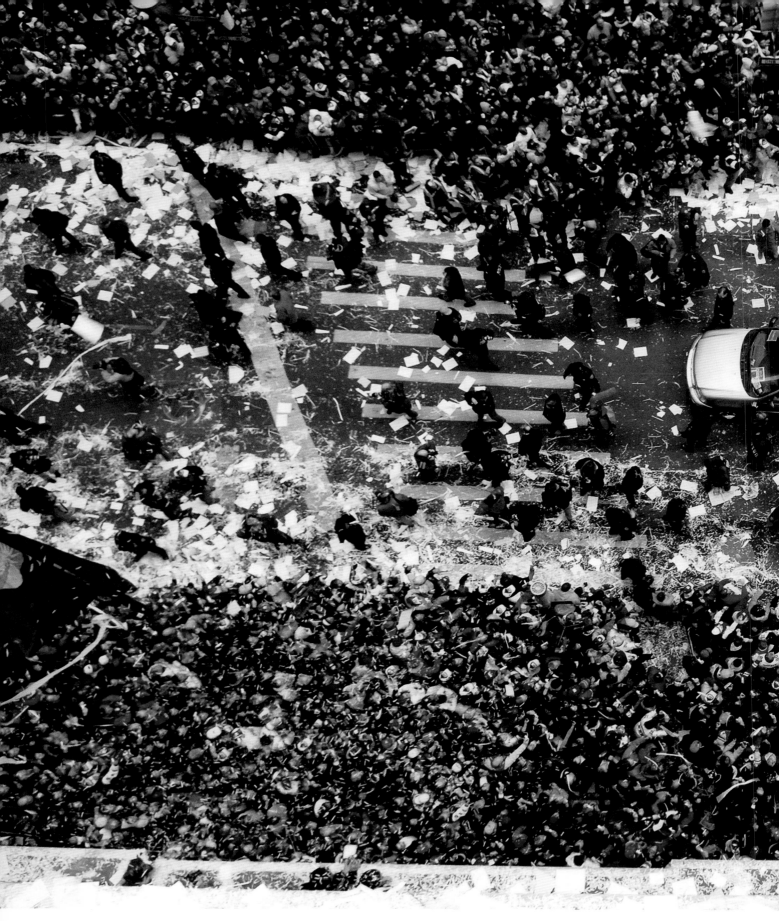

An aerial photo of the celebration on Broadway during the Giants' Super Bowl victory parade on Feb. 5, 2008.
Marc Hermann/Daily News

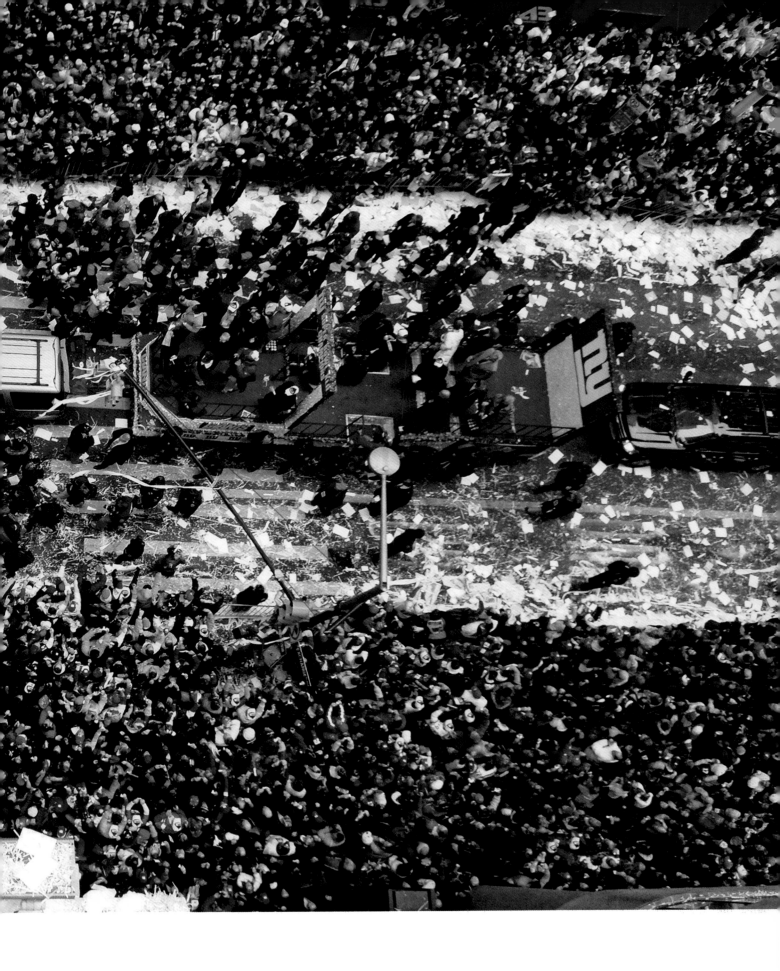

Brandon Jacobs (left) and Plaxico Burress (right) rejoice with Giants teammate David Tyree at the team's Super Bowl celebration at Giants Stadium on Feb. 5, 2008. *Howard Simmons/Daily News*

Giants quarterback Eli Manning holds up the Vince Lombardi trophy as he stands next to head coach Tom Coughlin following the Giants' win in Super Bowl XLII. *Linda Cataffo/Daily News*

DAILY ◎ NEWS

PUBLISHER: Mortimer Zuckerman
CHIEF EXECUTIVE OFFICER: Marc Z. Kramer
DEPUTY PUBLISHER AND EDITOR-IN-CHIEF: Martin Dunn
VICE PRESIDENT OF EDITORIAL ADMINISTRATION: Ed Fay
VICE PRESIDENT: Barry S. Surman
SPORTS EDITOR: Leon Carter
DIRECTOR OF PHOTOGRAPHY: Mike Lipack

PUBLISHERS: Peter L. Bannon and Joseph J. Bannon Sr.
SENIOR MANAGING EDITOR: Susan M. Moyer
COORDINATING EDITOR: Noah A. Amstadter
EDITOR: Doug Hoepker
ART DIRECTOR: Dustin Hubbart
BOOK LAYOUT: Dustin Hubbart and Doug Hoepker
IMAGING: Dustin Hubbart

Front cover photo by Howard Simmons/Daily News
Back cover photo by Linda Cataffo/Daily News

ISBN: 978-1-59670-308-7 (softcover edition)
978-1-59670-307-0 (hardcover edition)

Printed in the United States

Sports Publishing L.L.C.
804 North Neil Street
Champaign, IL 61820

Phone: 1-877-424-2665
Fax: 1-217-363-2073
Web site: www.SportsPublishingLLC.com

Giants fans celebrate the team's Super Bowl XLII victory at a ticker-tape parade in Manhattan on Feb. 5, 2008.
Andrew Savulich/Daily News

THE REAL PATRIOTS

19

Giants fans cheer the team on during the team's victory parade through Manhattan on Feb. 5, 2008. *Debbie Egan-Chin/Daily News*

BLUE MIRACLE

Giants wide receiver David Tyree pins the ball to his helmet as he catches a 32-yard pass from Eli Manning late in the fourth quarter of Super Bowl XLII. *Michael Appleton/Daily News*

A SEASON TO REMEMBER

February 11, 2008 ◆ By Ralph Vacchiano, Daily News

JOHN MARA WAS there at the end of the 1986 season to watch his father hold the Lombardi Trophy for the first time. He witnessed it again, in more dramatic fashion, at the end of the 1990 season.

Those were two of the most incredible moments in the storied history of the New York Giants. Yet there was Mara, standing on the podium in the middle of the Arizona desert on Feb. 3, 2008, declaring that there had never been a greater moment in the Giants' 83 years.

"I'll tell you what," the Giants' co-owner said after the Giants shocked the New England Patriots, 17-14, in Super Bowl XLII. "It's the greatest victory in the history of this franchise, without question."

Given a few hours, not much sleep, and one joyous postgame party to reconsider his words, Mara admitted to "wondering whether my emotions got the best of me at the time."

But he didn't wonder long.

"When you think about it, there were so many unique circumstances this year," Mara said. "And look at who we beat — a team everybody thought was going 19-0 and was going to be called 'The Greatest Team of All-Time.' And to come from where we came from?

"I just can't imagine any win in our history being bigger than that."

If nothing else, it was the most unexpected moment in Giants history. Just 13 months earlier they were coming off an ugly, turmoil-filled season that nearly resulted in the firing of Tom Coughlin. Their best player, Tiki Barber, retired at the end of the season. Their best defensive player, Michael Strahan, spent all of training camp contemplating packing it in.

Then the team started 0-2 and trailed 17-3 at halftime in Week 3 at Washington and all the bad memories came flooding back. Mara was depressed, anticipating the nightmare season that was unfolding. He turned to first-year general manager Jerry Reese and said "Jerry, I'm not sure how much more of this I can stand to watch."

Maybe the Giants needed to hit rock bottom before they could begin their ascent toward history, because it was at precisely that moment that the magic started to occur. The offense scored three unanswered touchdowns in the second half against the Redskins. The battered, beleaguered and bruised defense had a wondrous, last-second goal-line stand, which propelled the Giants on a six-game winning streak that set the stage for their miraculous postseason run.

Few believed in them, yet, however. How could they? The Giants couldn't even win at home (3-5). Eli Manning was as erratic as ever, even throwing a four-interception nightmare against the Vikings

Giants quarterback Eli Manning walks off the field following the Giants' upset victory over the Patriots.
Michael Appleton/Daily News

that led to him being called "Eli the Terrible" on the Daily News' back page. That's another reason what happened over the following nine weeks was so out of the blue.

"The guys on this team and the run we've made, it's hard to believe," Eli Manning said. "It really is."

You want unbelievable? How about the Giants beating the 18-0 Patriots, beating the great Tom Brady and the great Bill Belichick, right after that duo took a 14-10 lead with just

"THAT IS WHAT GOD DOES. HE MAKES SOME CRAZY THINGS HAPPEN."
—DAVID TYREE

2:42 left to play?

Manning's thought at that moment? "You like being down four when you know you have to score a touchdown to win the Super Bowl," said the kid they've always called Easy E. "You can't write a better script."

Then he went out and wrote one with one of the most memorable drives in Super Bowl history and a play Tom Coughlin said, "might be one of the great plays of all time in the

Super Bowl." Manning escaped a certain sack at the hands of two Patriots defenders, scrambled out of trouble and heaved a 32-yard pass to little-used receiver David Tyree, who outleaped a defender and used one hand to pin the ball to his helmet as he fell backwards.

Former GM Ernie Accorsi, who was watching from the stands, wiped a tear from his eye at that moment and thought, "They're not stopping us now."

Four plays later, Manning threw a 13-yard touchdown pass to Plaxico Burress. Thirty-five edge-of-your-seat seconds later, the Giants were the most unlikely of Super Bowl champs.

"Honestly, if you look at the road that we've been on this year, those are things that just don't make sense to the human mind," Tyree said. "That is what God does. He makes some crazy things happen."

Crazy. Wild. Incredible. Unbelievable. It's all nearly indescribable, even to those who thought they saw it coming. Like Accorsi, who one year earlier, upon his retirement, addressed the Giants at the end of their disappointing 2006 season and told them, "There's a championship in this room."

"I just didn't think it would be this soon," Accorsi said.

No one did. No one saw the 2007 Giants coming at all.

David Tyree (left) celebrates with Eli Manning following Tyree's fourth-quarter TD reception.
Corey Sipkin/Daily News

Michael Strahan shows off the Super Bowl trophy during the Giants' Parade of Champions in lower Manhattan. *Corey Sipkin/Daily News*

NEW YORK THROWS GIANT TICKER-TAPE PARADE

February 5, 2008 ◆ By Stephanie Gaskell and Corky Siemaszko, Daily News

NEW YORK WAS a glorious shade of Giants blue Tuesday as thousands of jubilant fans welcomed their conquering heroes home with a full-blown ticker-tape victory parade.

And no one expressed it better than Giants linebacker Michael Strahan, who capped the team's beatdown of the New England Patriots with a classic New York put down.

"We stomped you out!" Strahan declared on the steps of City Hall — punctuating it with a leap into the air.

Mayor Bloomberg, who hails from Boston, got into the spirit too with a put down of the Patriots, who were trying for a perfect 19-0 season when the Giants doused that dream on Sunday.

"The Giants may not be perfect, but then, no one is," Bloomberg said. "At least not this year in the NFL."

Super Bowl MVP Eli Manning — the team's resident shy guy — pumped a fist in the air as his float headed up Broadway, and smiled as delirious fans called out his name and a blizzard of confetti rained down from the gray skies.

"On behalf of this team I wanted to tell you how proud we are to bring a championship to New York City," Manning said at City Hall Plaza, where he and the other players were presented with keys to the city.

Some of the loudest applause was for David Tyree, who kept the Giants final scoring drive alive by catching a Manning pass — and holding it tightly against the back of his helmet — as he tumbled backward.

"He showed he could use his head," Bloomberg said.

The glorious cavalcade kicked off at 11 a.m. when the bells of Trinity Church near Wall Street sounded and soon they were drowned out by the

Confetti streams down to Broadway during the victory parade. *David Handschuh/Daily News*

ABOVE: Fans celebrate during the Giants victory parade. *All photos Andrew Savulich/Daily News*

cheers from the delirious crowd that echoed through the Canyon of Heroes.

The Giants faithful — many of whom had descended on downtown well before dawn to stake out primo spots on both sides of Broadway — cheered themselves hoarse.

Some brought footballs along and played catch with the players passing by on the floats.

It was the 177th ticker-tape parade up Broadway and the first since 2000, when the Yankees won the World Series. Crowd estimates were as high as 1 million people.

At some points the fans were 20 deep along the mile-long route where Charles Lindbergh and Apollo moon astronauts were feted in years past.

The Giants victory party was all-the-sweeter for Giants players and fans because nobody expected the Jints to make it to the Big Game — or beat the heavily favored Patriots.

Strahan flashed his famous gap-toothed grin and jumped up and down — with the coveted Vince Lombardi trophy in his hands — all the way from Battery Park to Chambers street while the adoring crowd went wild.

"Nobody believed, but New York believed and we believed," said Giants linebacker Antonio Pierce.

Along Broadway, the Giants faithful cheered "Eighteen and one! Eighteen and one!," mocking the Patriots, whose bid for a perfect season was undone by the Giants victory.

"It's huge," said Tommy Molinelli, a floor clerk at Radnor Research and Trading Co., who was wearing a red-and-blue Giants' sweatshirt. "The last time the Giants won the Super Bowl I was 17, now I'm 34. You never forget something like that."

Aeneas Carravetta, an advertizing consultant who works along the parade route, was supposed to be meeting with a customer. He rescheduled the meeting.

"You need to be down here with the people," said Carravetta, 26, of Long Island. "You only live once. You never know when this is going to happen again."

Steamfitter Richie Sanchez, who was working

Giants coach Tom Coughlin addresses the crowd at City Hall as his team cheers in the background.
Susan Watts/Daily News

on a building near Broadway, clambered up on the ladder he brought along for the job for a better view.

"This is a good view," he said. "This is history. I don't think my boss will mind. He's a Giants fan."

Fred Golini, 15, of Ronkonkoma, L.I., played hooky from school so he could take part in the Big Blue bash. He said he begged his parents who finally agreed after extracting from him a heavy price. "I have to do whatever they say for a while," he said.

"It's amazing for New York," Gov. Spitzer said. "I've never seen so many happy New Yorkers in one place."

Earlier, Giants owners Steve Tisch and John Mara helped ring the opening bell at the New York Stock Exchange. Workers on the exchange floor — many dressed in Giants jerseys — cheered as the bell sounded.

The Giants held another victory bash later at Giants Stadium in East Rutherford, N.J., the team's home field.

REGULAR SEASON

Cowboys cornerback Nathan Jones falls on Giants punter Jeff Feagles after a botched point-after attempt in the first quarter. *AP Images*

GIANTS POUNDED BY COWBOYS

September 10, 2007 ◆ By Ralph Vacchiano, Daily News

THE GIANTS DIDN'T just lose a game last night. They very nearly lost their season.

As it is, they will be holding their breath today awaiting the results on three critical MRIs — one on Osi Umenyiora's knee, another on Brandon Jacobs' knee and the big one on Eli Manning's right shoulder. All three players were casualties last night in the Giants' otherwise thrilling, season-opening, 45-35 loss to the Dallas Cowboys.

They lost Umenyiora on the first defensive series and Jacobs early in the second quarter. But the near-killer came with 7:20 left when, on a failed two-point conversion, Manning was slammed to the ground by rookie defensive end Anthony Spencer.

Manning got up and came back in to throw a touchdown pass to Plaxico Burress a few minutes later, pulling the Giants within 38-35. But he was unable to come back out with 2:54 remaining and the Giants down 10, leaving backup Jared Lorenzen to lead the desperation drive.

"It got a little tight and as time went on it got a little more sore," Manning said. "I didn't want to go in and make anything worse."

Manning had an otherwise spectacular night, completing 28 of 41 passes for 312 yards, four touchdowns (including three to Burress) and one interception that only happened because Burress slipped. He said he would have gone out for one more drive if the Giants were still within a touchdown.

"But when they got the final touchdown," he said, "I wanted to make the smart decision."

The final touchdown — a 51-yard pass from Tony Romo to Sam Hurd with 3:03 remaining — was the final nail in what Antonio Pierce called an "embarrassing" performance by the defense. After the Giants lost Umenyiora to a left knee injury in the first quarter, they struggled to generate a pass rush. That left the secondary exposed, and Romo (15-for-24, 345 yards, four touchdowns) ripped them apart.

He did most of his damage in the middle of the field, playing catch with tight end Jason Witten (6 catches, 116 yards, 1 touchdown). But he and Owens hooked up for two second-half scores, including a 47-yarder that gave the Cowboys a 38-22 lead early in the fourth.

The Cowboys scored four times in the second half and they burned the Giants for a total of 478 yards.

"We didn't get the pressure on the quarterback that we thought we were going to get," Tom Coughlin said. "When you rely on (an attacking) type of defense, you have to get to the quarterback. But that doesn't take away from the coverage aspect. The coverage was kind of baffling."

"It was obviously embarrassing for all of us," Pierce added. "The tackling, the coverage, everything. Nothing went well for us."

They had no such issues on offense, even after

New York receiver Plaxico Burress pulls in a 60-yard touchdown pass on the Giants' third play of the game. *AP Images*

they lost Jacobs to a sprained right MCL early in the second quarter when he appeared to awkwardly kick the back of Spencer on a two-yard run that was negated by a holding penalty on Chris Snee. At first, without Jacobs, the Giants had difficulty running the ball. But his replacement, third-year player Derrick Ward, eventually warmed up and finished with 13 carries for 89 yards.

And Manning — who hit Burress (8-144-3) for a 60-yard touchdown on the third play of the game — never stopped moving the ball. With the Giants trailing 17-6 late in the first half, he led a two-minute drive that resulted in Burress' second touchdown. And after the Cowboys fumbled the ensuing kickoff, they added the second of Lawrence Tynes' three field goals to pull within 17-16.

Then the second half became a shootout. Romo hit Owens for two scores and ran one in for himself, giving the Cowboys a 16-point lead

with 11:43 remaining. Manning answered with a a 9-yard pass to Ward with 7:20 remaining, pulling the Giants to within 38-28 (the two-point conversion try failed).

Still hurting, Manning said he "didn't really have any option" to sit out the next series after Gibril Wilson quickly picked off a Romo pass deep in Dallas territory. And he looked fine when he hit Burress in the back of the end zone from 10 yards out to make the score 38-35. Just 66 seconds later, Romo put the Giants out of their misery. All that was left was the body count.

And the count was undoubtedly high, though the extent of any of the injuries won't be known until today. Manning optimistically said he doesn't expect to miss any time.

"But we'll see how it feels (today)," he said. "We'll see what the X-rays and the MRIs say, and we'll go from there."

Cowboys running back Marion Barber is hit by Giants cornerback Sam Madison after crossing the goal line on an 18-yard run in the second quarter. *AP Images*

Giants running back Derrick Ward dives into the end zone for a touchdown in the fourth quarter. *AP Images*

WEEK 1

	1st	2nd	3rd	4th	Final
COWBOYS	3	14	14	14	45
GIANTS	6	10	3	16	35

Scoring Summary

1st
GIANTS   Plaxico Burress, 60 yd pass from Eli Manning, 13:31. Drive: 3 plays, 74 yards in 1:29.
COWBOYS   Nick Folk, 31 yd field goal, 06:32. Drive: 14 plays, 67 yards in 6:59.

2nd
COWBOYS   Marion Barber, 18 yd run (Nick Folk kick is good), 09:40. Drive: 5 plays, 56 yards in 2:21.
COWBOYS   Jason Witten, 12 yd pass from Tony Romo (Nick Folk kick is good), 03:59. Drive: 5 plays, 23 yards in 3:45.
GIANTS   Plaxico Burress, 4 yd pass from Eli Manning (Lawrence Tynes kick is good), 00:21. Drive: 12 plays, 75 yards in 3:38.
GIANTS   Lawrence Tynes, 44 yd field goal, 00:03.

3rd
COWBOYS   Terrell Owens, 22 yd pass from Tony Romo (Nick Folk kick is good), 12:00. Drive: 6 plays, 78 yards in 3:00.
GIANTS   Lawrence Tynes, 48 yd field goal, 05:47. Drive: 11 plays, 48 yards in 6:13.
COWBOYS   Tony Romo, 9 yd run (Nick Folk kick is good), 01:12. Drive: 4 plays, 67 yards in 1:56.

4th
GIANTS   Lawrence Tynes, 24 yd field goal, 13:23. Drive: 6 plays, 53 yards in 2:49.
COWBOYS   Terrell Owens, 47 yd pass from Tony Romo (Nick Folk kick is good), 11:43. Drive: 3 plays, 71 yards in 1:40.
GIANTS   Derrick Ward, 9 yd pass from Eli Manning (two-point conversion failed), 07:20. Drive: 9 plays, 80 yards in 4:23.
GIANTS   Plaxico Burress, 10 yd pass from Eli Manning (Lawrence Tynes kick is good), 04:09. Drive: 5 plays, 22 yards in 2:52.
COWBOYS   Sam Hurd, 51 yd pass from Tony Romo (Nick Folk kick is good), 03:03. Drive: 3 plays, 54 yards in 1:06.

Team Stats

	COWBOYS	GIANTS
1st Downs	21	22
3rd-Down Conversions	6-11	7-14
4th-Down Conversions	2-2	0-2
Punts-Average	2-54.0	2-44.5
Punts-Returns	2-15	1-13
Kickoffs-Returns	7-182	7-193
Interceptions-Returns	1-18	1-10
Penalties-Yards	7-55	4-45
Fumbles-Lost	1-1	1-0
Time of Possession	27:57	32:03
Total Net Yards	478	438
Total Plays	55	67
Net Yards Rushing	142	124
Rushes	30	22
Net Yards Passing	336	314
Comp.-Att.-Int.	14-24-1	29-44-1
Sacked-Yards Lost	1-9	1-5
Red Zone Efficiency	3/4-75%	3/4-75%

Packers safety Atari Bigby tries to tackle tight end Jeremy Shockey. *Lee Weissman/Daily News*

GIANTS COLLAPSE IN ALL PHASES

September 17, 2007 ◆ by Ralph Vacchiano, Daily News

ELI MANNING DID all he could, turning in a gutty performance just one week after spraining his right shoulder. It was just too much to ask him to have to shoulder the defense, too.

For the second week in a row, it was the defense that doomed the Giants, as they dropped their home opener to the Green Bay Packers yesterday, 35-13. While getting off to their first 0-2 start since 1996, the Giants have given up 846 total yards, 621 passing yards and a ridiculous 80 points.

The Giants hadn't given up that many points in back to back games since 1973. And to find a worst defensive performance in the first two games of the season, you have to go all the way back to 1966.

"I think we're a better football team than we showed," Tom Coughlin said. "Obviously I don't have any real grounds for saying that."

Well, there was the solid performance by Manning, who completed 16 of 29 passes for 211 yards with one touchdown and one interception. Beyond that, Coughlin was right: There wasn't much evidence that the Giants (0-2) are a better team.

The defense was, once again, defenseless. The

> "I THINK WE'RE A BETTER FOOTBALL TEAM THAN WE SHOWED."
> —TOM COUGHLIN

pass rush was nonexistent. And while the coverage wasn't necessarily "baffling," as Coughlin called it last week, it wasn't exactly tight as eight different receivers caught passes from Brett Favre.

Favre (29-for-38, 286 yards, three touchdowns, one interception) opened the second half by completing 14 consecutive passes, completing the streak with a three-yard touchdown pass to tight end David Lee in the fourth quarter that gave Green Bay (2-0) a 21-13 lead. Favre added one more touchdown pass on his way to his NFL record 149th career victory, as the Packers used 21 fourth-quarter points to pull away.

The Giants, as usual, helped — and not just with a porous defense. After Favre's first touchdown pass, Manning drove to the Packers' 8, but they had to settle for a field goal after a killer 15-yard taunting penalty was called on mild-mannered receiver Amani Toomer. A similar thing happened to them in the first half when Jeremy Shockey short-circuited a drive by drawing a five-yard delay of game penalty for spiking the ball after a first-down catch near the Packers 15.

The Giants had to settle for one of Lawrence

Packers safety Atari Bigby breaks up a pass intended for Jeremy Shockey, who finished with 60 receiving yards. *Lee Weissman/Daily News*

WEEK 2

	1st	2nd	3rd	4th	Final
PACKERS	0	7	7	21	35
GIANTS	0	10	3	0	13

Scoring Summary

2nd
PACKERS DeShawn Wynn, 6 yd run (Mason Crosby kick is good), 08:18. Drive: 6 plays, 71 yards in 3:13.
GIANTS Plaxico Burress, 26 yd pass from Eli Manning (Lawrence Tynes kick is good), 07:16. Drive: 2 plays, 66 yards in 1:02.
GIANTS Lawrence Tynes, 48 yd field goal, 01:38. Drive: 8 plays, 41 yards in 3:46.

3rd
PACKERS Bubba Franks, 2 yd pass from Brett Favre (Mason Crosby kick is good), 09:07. Drive: 10 plays, 51 yards in 5:53.
GIANTS Lawrence Tynes, 32 yd field goal, 04:22. Drive: 10 plays, 49 yards in 4:45.

4th
PACKERS Donald Lee, 3 yd pass from Brett Favre (Mason Crosby kick is good), 13:33. Drive: 10 plays, 80 yards in 5:49.
PACKERS Donald Driver, 10 yd pass from Brett Favre (Mason Crosby kick is good), 11:41. Drive: 5 plays, 22 yards in 1:45.
PACKERS DeShawn Wynn, 38 yd run (Mason Crosby kick is good), 04:12. Drive: 5 plays, 53 yards in 2:23.

Team Stats

	PACKERS	GIANTS
1st Downs	25	20
3rd-Down Conversions	6-11	5-12
4th-Down Conversions	0-0	0-1
Punts-Average	3-36.0	3-43.7
Punts-Returns	2-8	1-2
Kickoffs-Returns	3-83	5-105
Interceptions-Returns	1-9	1-0
Penalties-Yards	8-63	6-71
Fumbles-Lost	0-0	2-1
Time of Possession	34:26	25:34
Total Net Yards	368	325
Total Plays	68	58
Net Yards Rushing	83	94
Rushes	29	16
Net Yards Passing	285	231
Comp.-Att.-Int.	29-38-1	20-40-1
Sacked-Yards Lost	1-1	2-13
Red Zone Efficiency	4/4-100%	0/3-0%

Tynes' two field goals (48, 32) there, too.

"We know better than that," Manning said. "These guys know better than that."

"We made some stupid penalties," Coughlin added. "We have no excuses. There's no explanation for it. We gave ourselves some opportunities and that took it away. We became our own worst enemy, at least for a while."

There were other gaffes too, like when rookie Ahmad Bradshaw fumbled a kickoff return, setting up Favre's final touchdown pass, a 10-yard strike to Donald Driver. But their real worst enemy has been new defensive coordinator Steve Spagnuolo's defense, which is supposed to be aggressive and attacking but so far has been neither. In two games, the Giants have two sacks — both by Justin Tuck. And like Cowboys quarterback Tony Romo one week ago, Favre was hardly hit or hurried.

That was most evident in the second half when he broke open a game with 14 consecutive completions, including a two-yard touchdown pass to Bubba Franks and the fourth-quarter one to Lee. In the second half, Favre was 18-for-21 for three touchdowns and 147 yards.

"It's just frustrating," said defensive tackle Barry Cofield. "He's in a rhythm and he's doing what he wants. That's about as bad as you can imagine."

And with not much of a pass rush, that left the Giants' secondary exposed for Driver (eight catches, 73 yards) and James Jones (4-75).

"Obviously there was some elusiveness that we didn't necessarily contend with," Coughlin said.

Manning deserved much better. Shaking off an injury that he finally admitted doctors had told him would likely keep him out "a few games," he made some impressive throws. His touchdown came on a two-play, 66-yard series that featured one 40-yard pass to Toomer and a 26-yard touchdown pass to Plaxico Burress that he somehow fit in just over the hands of Packers safety Atari Bigby.

On the next drive, right after Shockey's spiking penalty, Manning scrambled right and made a throw across his body and back across the field that Shockey dropped inside the 5. In the third quarter, he just missed hitting Toomer in the end zone from 21 yards away on a pass that was just a bit too high.

In the end, though, it only amounted to 13 points, which wasn't enough for a defense that is beginning to look like one of the worst in the league.

"We're not going to get any worse," vowed defensive end Osi Umenyiora. "I'm not saying I'll guarantee we're going to win the game (Sunday in Washington), but I guarantee we'll play better."

"We've got to fix it and fix it fast," added cornerback Sam Madison. "If not we're going to just keep running down hill."

Packers running back DeShawn Wynn is tackled by an army of Giants defenders.
Michael Appleton/Daily News

Redskins quarterback Jason Campbell is tackled by Giants cornerback Aaron Ross during the third quarter.
AP Images

GIANTS' DEFENSE SEALS COMEBACK WIN

September 24, 2007 ◆ By Ralph Vacchiano, Daily News

MAYBE THE AIR horn Antonio Pierce blew in the locker room last week was a wake-up call, after all.

Something certainly got the attention of the Giants' beleaguered defense, which was literally pushed to within a yard yesterday of possibly seeing the entire season slip away. With 58 seconds to go, the Washington Redskins had four chances to go one yard and tie the ballgame.

It was a yard the defense knew the Redskins were never going to get.

"We had already decided there was no way we were going to play that good in the first 58 minutes and let it slip away on the last drive," said defensive end Justin Tuck. "We said, 'No way are they going to score. If they get to the one-inch line they're not going to score.'"

The record shows that safety James Butler made the final tackle on Ladell Betts to preserve the Giants' come-from-behind, 24-17 victory, but it was Tuck who got his arm out just enough to stop him.

> "WE KNEW SOONER OR LATER (THE OFFENSE WAS) GOING TO GET IT GOING. WE JUST HAD TO KEEP DOING WHAT WE WERE DOING."
> —OSI UMENYIORA

The real credit belonged to the entire unit anyway, especially after how they had become the butt of jokes in the first two weeks of the season. They played well the entire game, but they absolutely shut down the Redskins after halftime, allowing only 63 yards in the second half.

That gave a shaky offense enough time to get itself on track and score 21 unanswered points in the final two quarters. The final seven came with 5:32 remaining, when Plaxico Burress took a short pass from Eli Manning, made two defenders miss and turned it into a 33-yard, game-winning touchdown.

To say it was a must-win would be an understatement, since a loss by the Giants (1-2) would've left them three games behind the Redskins (2-1). "That probably would be the end of our season right there," Tuck said.

But despite their dire situation, the mood at halftime was oddly upbeat, even though the Giants trailed 17-3. They knew both Redskins' scores — a 1-yard run by Clinton Portis (14 carries, 60 yards) and an 8-yard touchdown pass from Jason Campbell (16-for-34, 190 yards) to tight end Chris Cooley — were the direct results of turnovers by Manning. He was having an off day thanks in part to drops from his receivers. He fumbled once and threw interceptions twice.

"We knew sooner or later they were going to get it going," said defensive end Osi Umenyiora. "We just had to keep doing what we were doing."

"We knew with one score it was a 17-10 game," said Tom Coughlin. "And we were right back in it."

Manning (21-for-36, 232 yards) did just that on the first drive of the first half, when he led the Giants to a 1-yard Reuben Droughns touchdown. Droughns would add another, tying the game with 12:33 left in the fourth quarter while the Giants' defense was in the process of forcing three straight three-and-outs.

Then came what should have been the play of the game — a fumbled handoff by Portis that was recovered by Pierce, who was unusually (and purposefully) quiet after the game. Four plays later, Manning and Burress (five catches, 86 yards, all in the second half) connected for the game-winning touchdown.

The defense, though, had a few more big plays to go.

First they stopped what seemed to be the Redskins' final drive at the Giants' 35 with 2:50 remaining. But a three-and-out by the Giants and a 27-yard punt return by Antwaan Randle El gave the Redskins the ball at the Giants' 35 again with 2:19 remaining. With the help of a 15-yard, fourth-and-8 pass from Campbell to Santana Moss, the Redskins eventually had a first-and-goal at the 1 with less than a minute to go.

The defense again had the game and the season in its hands.

"That's what we asked for at halftime," Pierce said. "It happened to come out that way."

On the first play, Campbell spiked the ball — an odd decision with 51 seconds remaining. On the second play, his short pass to fullback Mike Sellers was too low.

The next two plays were runs by Betts toward the left, away from Michael Strahan and right at Umenyiora and Tuck, who was in at defensive tackle.

"We enjoyed the fact that they're picking on us," Tuck said. "I guess they think we can't stop the run."

They were wrong. So was anyone who counted out this Giants defense.

"We needed it, man," Strahan said. "Thank God we played like we needed it and wanted it. For us, a stop like that, it was a lot of emotion, a lot of relief for this team."

"To win a game like this when we needed it, on the fourth-down play on our goal line," Tuck added, "you can't write a story any better than that."

WEEK 3

	1st	2nd	3rd	4th	Final
REDSKINS	7	10	0	0	17
GIANTS	3	0	7	14	24

Scoring Summary

1st
GIANTS Lawrence Tynes, 34 yd field goal, 7:19. Drive: 9 plays, 54 yards in 3:29.
REDSKINS Clinton Portis, 1 yd run (Shaun Suisham kick is good), 4:57. Drive: 2 plays, 6 yards in 0:40.

2nd
REDSKINS Chris Cooley, 8 yd pass from Jason Campbell (Shaun Suisham kick is good), 7:55. Drive: 7 plays, 72 yards in 4:16.
REDSKINS Shaun Suisham, 47 yd field goal, 0:00. Drive: 4 plays, 5 yards in 1:33.

3rd
GIANTS Reuben Droughns, 1 yd run (Lawrence Tynes kick is good), 9:50. Drive: 10 plays, 61 yards in 5:10.

4th
GIANTS Reuben Droughns, 1 yd run (Lawrence Tynes kick is good), 12:33. Drive: 11 plays, 62 yards in 6:11.
GIANTS Plaxico Burress, 33 yd pass from Eli Manning (Lawrence Tynes kick is good), 5:32. Drive: 4 plays, 44 yards in 2:01.

Team Stats

	REDSKINS	GIANTS
1st Downs	14	19
3rd-Down Conversions	5-16	9-16
4th-Down Conversions	1-2	0-0
Punts-Average	7-45.4	5-39.2
Punts-Returns	3-36	3-23
Kickoffs-Returns	5-140	3-76
Interceptions-Returns	2-9	0-0
Penalties-Yards	6-37	3-15
Fumbles-Lost	3-1	1-1
Time of Possession	27:02	32:58
Total Net Yards	260	315
Total Plays	63	68
Net Yards Rushing	82	96
Rushes	27	30
Net Yards Passing	178	219
Comp.-Att.-Int.	16-34-0	21-36-2
Sacked-Yards Lost	2-12	2-13
Red Zone Efficiency	2/4-50%	2/3-66%

Giants wide receiver Plaxico Burress runs upfield on a 33-yard touchdown reception to give New York a fourth-quarter lead. *AP Images*

Eagles quarterback Donovan McNabb is sacked by New York's Justin Tuck. *Lee Weissman/Daily News*

GIANTS DEFENSE GROUNDS DONOVAN McNABB, EAGLES

October 1, 2007 ◆ by Ralph Vacchiano, Daily News

THERE HAVE BEEN a lot of great defensive performances inside Giants Stadium — even a few by the players on the current Giants.

But none of them have ever seen anything like what they saw last night.

Right from the start, the Giants were all over Eagles quarterback Donovan McNabb like a swarm of hungry bees, and when it was all over they had tied an NFL record with 12 sacks — including a team-record six from Osi Umenyiora. The barrage left the Philadelphia Eagles, who were coming off a 56-point explosion a week ago, dazed and confused after a 16-3 Giants win.

"I was amazed," said linebacker Kawika Mitchell, who returned a fumble 17 yards for a touchdown to ice it in the third quarter. "It was definitely one to remember."

"I'm going all the way back to Pop Warner," added linebacker Antonio Pierce. "I've never seen anything like that."

Nobody saw this one coming, even after the Giants' impressive defensive effort one week earlier at Washington. This was the same unit that ranked 29th in the league after giving up 80 points in the first two weeks of the season. And even in the Redskins game they only had two sacks, giving them just four on the season.

Last night, they sacked McNabb five times in the first half.

"We have some of the best pass rushers in the league on this team," Umenyiora said. "We just hadn't put it all together yet."

Umenyiora led the way, abusing left tackle Winston Justice, a second-year player filling in for injured starter William Thomas. Justice gave up five of Umenyiora's six sacks. They got three more from much-maligned linebacker Mathias Kiwanuka. Justin Tuck, their best defensive player the first three weeks, chipped in with two. And Michael Strahan finally got the one that broke his tie with Lawrence Taylor atop the Giants' all-time list with 133-½ for his career.

Given little time to throw, and with running back Brian Westbrook out with an abdominal strain, McNabb looked lost, completing just 15 of 31 passes for 138 yards.

"That was the Giants defense in action," Tom Coughlin said.

Its timing couldn't have been better, for a variety of reasons. It was defensive coordinator Steve Spagnuolo's first game against the team he worked for from 1999-2006, and he dazzled the Eagles with an array of blitzes. He confused them further by using Umenyiora and Tuck at linebacker, as well as Kiwanuka along the defensive line.

The performance also came in the presence of greatness. The famed "Crunch Bunch" — linebackers Lawrence Taylor, Harry Carson, Brian

Giants defensive end Michael Strahan pumps his fist after recording his franchise record-setting 133-½ career sack. *Michael Appleton/Daily News*

Kelley and Brad Van Pelt — was introduced before the game. "To have a game like that in front of those guys is something to be proud of," Pierce said.

The Giants evened their record at 2-2, allowing them to keep pace with the Dallas Cowboys (4-0). The defense's performance came on a night when Eli Manning (14-for-26, 135 yards, one touchdown, one interception) was shaky and the offense was held to 212 total yards.

The only scoring the offense contributed was a 9-yard touchdown pass from Manning to Plaxico Burress in the first half and a 29-yard field goal by Lawrence Tynes in the third quarter. The other six points came on Mitchell's fumble return for a score.

That was more than enough for a defense that surrendered only a 53-yard field goal in the fourth quarter by David Akers that broke its shutout string at 77:09.

"It was an outstanding defensive effort," Coughlin said. "Just continuous pressure on the quarterback, a defensive touchdown — all the things you think about when you think about a great defensive game."

The star of the show was Umenyiora, who didn't have a sack in the first three games. He was so hungry for one that in the trainer's room before the game he came up with the Giants' new sack celebration — miming the motion of a spoon to their mouths, which goes with the new motto, "Let's eat."

Giants wide receiver Plaxico Burress celebrates after putting New York on the board with a touchdown in the second quarter. *Michael Appleton/Daily News*

Giants linebacker Kawika Mitchell carries the ball for a 17-yard touchdown run after picking up an Eagles fumble in the third quarter. *Michael Appleton/Daily News*

On the sidelines, Umenyiora's teammates told him, "It's like a video game for you out there."

"Of course it wasn't," he said. "Tonight was just one of those nights."

"We call him 'The Great One,'" Pierce said. "Today he was 'The Great One.' He needed an IV at halftime he was rushing so hard. Really, he dominated the game by himself."

"I've never seen someone go from last in the league to probably leading the league in sacks in one game," Strahan added. "He deserved every one of them."

WEEK 4

	1st	2nd	3rd	4th	Final
EAGLES	0	0	0	3	3
GIANTS	0	7	9	0	16

Scoring Summary
2nd
GIANTS Plaxico Burress, 9 yd pass from Eli Manning (Lawrence Tynes kick is good), 11:09. Drive: 4 plays, 49 yards in 1:55.

3rd
GIANTS Lawrence Tynes, 29 yd field goal, 2:03. Drive: 6 plays, 55 yards in 2:59.
GIANTS Kawika Mitchell, 17 yd fumble kick failed, 1:30.

4th
EAGLES David Akers, 53 yd field goal, 12:51. Drive: 10 plays, 40 yards in 3:39.

Team Stats

	EAGLES	GIANTS
1st Downs	16	16
3rd-Down Conversions	5-16	3-11
4th-Down Conversions	0-1	0-0
Punts-Average	8-41.6	6-37.2
Punts-Returns	3-20	5-41
Kickoffs-Returns	4-98	1-32
Interceptions-Returns	1-49	0-0
Penalties-Yards	15-132	4-27
Fumbles-Lost	4-1	0-0
Time of Possession	30:26	29:34
Total Net Yards	190	212
Total Plays	66	54
Net Yards Rushing	114	83
Rushes	23	27
Net Yards Passing	76	129
Comp.-Att.-Int.	15-31-0	14-26-1
Sacked-Yards Lost	12-61	1-6
Red Zone Efficiency	0/1-0%	1/4-25%

Rookie cornerback Aaron Ross leaps to make his first of two crucial, second-half interceptions against the Jets. *Michael Appleton/Daily News*

GIANTS GROUND JETS IN SECOND HALF

October 8, 2007 ◆ By Ralph Vacchiano, Daily News

WHILE THE DEFENSE carried the Giants through their resurgence, the offense remained confident it would be ready when needed.

Yesterday, in the second half against the Jets, it finally flipped the switch on.

"They can do that, and that's the scary thing," said linebacker Antonio Pierce. "Really, that's been our whole team's motto: Whenever we decide we're going to do something, we get it done."

The Giants decided to play just in time to explode for 28 second-half points and rally from a 10-point deficit to beat the Jets, 35-24, at Giants Stadium. They earned New York bragging rights with a terrific 53-yard touchdown catch by Plaxico Burress in the fourth quarter, and sealed them when rookie corner Aaron Ross rebounded from a surprise benching with a 43-yard interception return for a touchdown with 3:15 to go.

The win was the third straight for the Giants (3-2) after an 0-2 start and kept them in contention in the NFC East. It also left their cross-stadium rivals demoralized with a record of 1-4.

"Teams have gotten out of it (before)," said Jets safety Kerry Rhodes. "We would like to think that we are one of those teams."

The Jets held a 17-7 lead at halftime, holding Eli Manning to 22 passing yards. They took advantage of a gift to score their first touchdown — a fumble by Brandon Jacobs on his second carry since miss-ing the last three weeks with a sprained knee. He was stripped by Rhodes, who scooped up the ball and carried it 11 yards into the end zone.

The Giants handed the Jets three more points at the end of the half when, after a 16-yard touchdown pass from Chad Pennington to Brad Smith put the Jets up 14-7, the Giants came out throwing from their own 21 with 28 seconds remaining. That ill-advised call led to an interception by Jonathan Vilma that set up Mike Nugent's 47-yard field goal that gave the Jets their 17-7 halftime lead.

"We had a lot of things go against us," Tom Coughlin said. "Our theme is always, 'Don't beat yourself,' and we put ourselves in a bad hole that way."

They continued to dig that hole into the third quarter. After capping an 80-yard drive on Jacobs' 19-yard touchdown run to open the second half, they allowed Leon Washington's 98-yard return for a touchdown on the ensuing kickoff.

"In the first half we couldn't get anything going," said Manning, who was 10-of-15 for 164 yards in the second half and 13-for-25, 186 yards total. "Then it kind of kick-started. We got something going. We made some adjustments, picked them up and were able to throw the ball down-field."

Before the end of the third quarter, Manning led

the Giants on a 68-yard drive that ended with a 13-yard touchdown pass to Jeremy Shockey, the brash tight end's first of the season. And on the next drive, Ross — who sat the entire first half for what Coughlin said was "a violation of team rules" — picked off a Pennington pass at the Giants' 2-yard line.

From there, the Giants marched 98 yards for the go-ahead score, with a little help from Jets line-backer David Harris, who drew a 15-yard penalty for a horse-collar tackle on Giants running back Derrick Ward. Two plays later, Manning threw a quick out to Burress (five catches, 124 yards), who caught the ball at the Jets' 47, stiff-armed cornerback Andre Dyson, and took off down the sideline for a touchdown that gave the Giants their first lead, 28-24.

"If you are going to win some of these tight games, guys are going to have to step up and make a play when it's available," Manning said. "And that's what he did. He did something a little extra. That's a big play by him."

The Jets and Pennington, whose job security is now in question after his three-interception performance, didn't have any big plays left in them. But the Giants had one more — when Ross stepped in front of Jerricho Cotchery and raced 43 yards for the final touchdown of the game.

"We play when we have to," Burress said. "It shouldn't be that way all the time. We should beat the bad teams by a lot and beat the good teams by a little. We needed to have that attitude not just when we have to play. We need to have that attitude from the start."

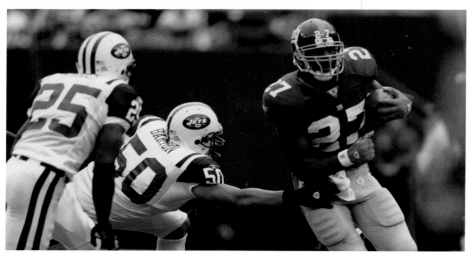

Brandon Jacobs carried the ball 20 times for the Giants and racked up 100 yards rushing and one TD. *Michael Appleton/Daily News*

WEEK 5

	1st	2nd	3rd	4th	Final
JETS	7	10	7	0	24
GIANTS	0	7	14	14	35

Scoring Summary

1st
JETS — Kerry Rhodes, 11 yd fumble (Mike Nugent kick is good), 8:36.

2nd
GIANTS — Derrick Ward, 8 yd run (Lawrence Tynes kick is good), 10:54. Drive: 9 plays, 67 yards in 5:29.
JETS — Brad Smith, 16 yd pass from Chad Pennington (Mike Nugent kick is good), 0:33. Drive: 9 plays, 93 yards in 1:46.
JETS — Mike Nugent, 47 yd field goal, 0:00.

3rd
GIANTS — Brandon Jacobs, 19 yd run (Lawrence Tynes kick is good), 11:17. Drive: 6 plays, 80 yards in 3:43.
JETS — Leon Washington, 98 yd kick return (Mike Nugent kick is good), 11:03.
GIANTS — Jeremy Shockey, 13 yd pass from Eli Manning (Lawrence Tynes kick is good), 0:33. Drive: 9 plays, 68 yards in 5:06.

4th
GIANTS — Plaxico Burress, 53 yd pass from Eli Manning (Lawrence Tynes kick is good), 7:52. Drive: 8 plays, 98 yards in 4:31.
GIANTS — Aaron Ross, 43 yd interception return (Lawrence Tynes kick is good), 3:15.

Team Stats

	JETS	GIANTS
1st Downs	16	21
3rd-Down Conversions	9-15	5-12
4th-Down Conversions	0-1	1-1
Punts-Average	4-45.3	5-46.8
Punts-Returns	2-20	2-16
Kickoffs-Returns	5-200	3-62
Interceptions-Returns	1-1	3-68
Penalties-Yards	6-40	3-37
Fumbles-Lost	0-0	1-1
Time of Possession	26:15	33:45
Total Net Yards	277	374
Total Plays	62	64
Net Yards Rushing	55	188
Rushes	25	39
Net Yards Passing	222	186
Comp.-Att.-Int.	21-36-3	13-25-1
Sacked-Yards Lost	1-7	0-0
Red Zone Efficiency	1/1-100%	3/4-75%

Jeremy Shockey scores on a 13-yard reception from Eli Manning late in the third quarter.
Michael Appleton/Daily News

Giants wide receiver Plaxico Burress had six receptions for 97 yards, including a 43-yard TD reception.
AP Images

GIANTS BLOW OUT FALCONS

October 16, 2007 ◆ By Ralph Vacchiano, Daily News

THERE WAS NO need for a big second-half comeback or any late-game heroics against the Atlanta Falcons last night. This time, Eli Manning didn't save his best for last.

In a reversal of fortune, the Giants got off to the fast start they have been craving, thanks mostly to a brilliant first half by Manning, and rode it all the way to their fourth straight win, a 31-10 victory over the Atlanta Falcons. Manning got the Giants going by completing nearly 70% of his first-half passes inside the Georgia Dome, including a career-best streak of 12 in row.

"It was impressive," Tom Coughlin said. "He had the hot hand, no doubt about it."

"We wanted to set the tone for the game," added receiver Amani Toomer. "That's the first time this year we actually did that."

Manning ended up completing 27 of 39 passes for 303 yards, two touchdowns and two interceptions — easily his best game since opening night. And even when he slowed down in the second half — completing only 10-of-14 for 95 yards and one interception — he was picked up by a rushing attack that gained 188 yards for the second consecutive week.

The defense chipped in too, taking advantage of the Falcons' two backup tackles and sacking hapless Falcons quarterback Joey Harrington (18-for-39, 209 yards) four times. They also all but shut down the Falcons' rushing attack, with the notable exception of one 67-yard touchdown run by Jerious Norwood in the first quarter.

It was a thorough performance all around and good enough to boost the Giants to a 4-2 record and into second place in the NFC East, just a game behind the Dallas Cowboys (5-1).

Suddenly, 0-2 seems like eons ago.

"It feels pretty good," said defensive end Osi Umenyiora. "We've still got a long ways to go. But if we keep playing the way we're playing, I think we've got a chance to do something special."

Even last night, though, the Giants needed a boost. When their first drive appeared to stall after three plays, the Falcons kept the Giants alive with a dumb roughing-the-kicker penalty that came when Demorrio Williams ran into punter Jeff Feagles. Eight plays later, Manning faked a handoff to Brandon Jacobs and hit Toomer over the middle for a 5-yard touchdown and a 7-3 Giants lead.

As good as Manning was, though, the Giants kept trying to give the game back. On the first play of the Falcons' next drive, Norwood took off for his long touchdown, putting the Falcons up 10-7. And though the Giants quickly answered with a 1-yard touchdown by Reuben Droughns (14 carries, 90 yards), they gave the Falcons a huge chance to get back in it on the next series when ex-Jet defensive end John Abraham forced a Manning fumble

Giants tight end Jeremy Shockey contributed to a balanced aerial attack with 63 yards receiving. *AP Images*

WEEK 6 ....

	1st	2nd	3rd	4th	Final
FALCONS	10	0	0	0	10
GIANTS	14	7	0	10	31

Scoring Summary
1st
FALCONS Morten Andersen, 47 yd field goal, 11:47. Drive: 8 plays, 41 yards in 3:13.
GIANTS Amani Toomer, 5 yd pass from Eli Manning (Lawrence Tynes kick is good), 5:32. Drive: 11 plays, 73 yards in 6:15.
FALCONS Jerious Norwood, 67 yd run (Morten Andersen kick is good), 5:14. Drive: 1 play, 67 yards in 0:18.
GIANTS Reuben Droughns, 1 yd run (Lawrence Tynes kick is good), 2:13. Drive: 6 plays, 82 yards in 3:01.
2nd
GIANTS Plaxico Burress, 43 yd pass from Eli Manning (Lawrence Tynes kick is good), 8:21. Drive: 4 plays, 62 yards in 2:22.
4th
GIANTS Lawrence Tynes, 32 yd field goal, 10:52. Drive: 13 plays, 79 yards in 7:57.
GIANTS Derrick Ward, 9 yd run (Lawrence Tynes kick is good), 3:08. Drive: 4 plays, 67 yards in 1:42.

Team Stats
	FALCONS	GIANTS
1st Downs	14	28
3rd-Down Conversions	3-13	6-14
4th-Down Conversions	0-1	1-1
Punts-Average	7-41.1	4-39.5
Punts-Returns	1-7	1-10
Kickoffs-Returns	6-105	3-70
Interceptions-Returns	2-45	1-8
Penalties-Yards	3-31	6-45
Fumbles-Lost	0-0	1-1
Time of Possession	20:22	39:38
Total Net Yards	284	491
Total Plays	58	75
Net Yards Rushing	103	188
Rushes	15	35
Net Yards Passing	181	303
Comp.-Att.-Int.	18-39-1	27-39-2
Sacked-Yards Lost	4-28	1-0
Red Zone Efficiency	0/0-0%	3/4-75%

that the Falcons recovered on the Giants' 28.

But the Falcons couldn't capitalize, and by then, Manning was rolling. After a missed 48-yard field goal by 47-year-old Morten Andersen, Manning connected with a mostly uncovered Plaxico Burress on a 43-yard touchdown pass that gave the Giants a 21-10 lead. The touchdown was Manning's 11th straight completion.

That seemed to be the end of Manning's magic, though. He was picked off with about 17 seconds left in the first half, though once again the Falcons couldn't capitalize. And in the third quarter he just couldn't seem to get the offense moving, despite getting an enormous break from the officials.

On first down from the Giants' 25, Manning hit Burress with a short pass that he appeared to hold for several seconds before Falcons cornerback DeAngelo Hall stripped it away. Hall probably would have recovered the loose ball and scored a touchdown if the referees hadn't blown the play dead and ruled it an incomplete pass.

"I caught the ball and (Hall) was poking at it and I couldn't tuck it away," Burress said. "I'm just glad they didn't throw the red flag (calling for a review)."

Regardless, the Giants still did their best to keep the Falcons alive — this time when Hall picked off a deep pass from Manning inside the Falcons' 10 later in that same drive and returned it all the way back across midfield. It was the story of the game — and probably the season — for 1-5 Atlanta: They couldn't turn the turnover into points.

And while the Giants' defense held, the running game did what it does best — it wore down the Falcons' defense. Droughns and Jacobs (13-86) did most of the work because Derrick Ward was nursing an ankle injury. But Ward was healthy enough to return in time to seal the game with a 9-yard touchdown run with 3:08 to play.

Giants receiver Amani Toomer celebrates after catching a 5-yard TD pass from Eli Manning in the first quarter. *AP Images*

Michael Strahan celebrates after a sack in the second quarter. The Giants collected six sacks and two interceptions against the 49ers. *Michael Appleton/Daily News*

GIANTS DEFENSE BATTERS 49ERS

October 22, 2007 ◆ By Ralph Vacchiano, Daily News

THE GIANTS' PASS rush has become so relentless that opposing quarterbacks now seem to feel the pressure before kickoff. By the time the game starts, the Giants' defense can see the fear in their eyes.

"We like to think that they come into the game uncomfortable," said linebacker Mathias Kiwanuka. "When you get out there and start getting into their face, you can definitely understand that it's going to affect them a little bit. You're going to get them on their heels, out of rhythm, out of sync."

That was an apt way to describe the San Francisco 49ers and embattled quarterback Trent Dilfer, who was pummeled for six sacks and turned the ball over four times yesterday. The Giants turned those giveaways into a field goal and three touchdowns, including a 75-yard fumble return by Osi Umenyiora, on their way to an easy 33-15 win at the Meadowlands.

It was the fifth straight win for the Giants and the fifth consecutive outstanding performance by their rising and confident defense. The win kept the Giants (5-2) on the heels of the Dallas Cowboys, one game back in the NFC East.

For that they can thank their defense, which gave the offense a chance to take a more methodical approach — pounding the ball on the ground (140 rushing yards, including a career-high 107 from Brandon Jacobs) to supplement a short-passing attack. Eli Manning was just 18-of-31 for 146 yards, despite being the victim of five dropped passes.

Most importantly, he capitalized on the big plays by the defense and only made one mistake.

That mistake — a first-quarter interception on a pass that was tipped at the line of scrimmage — turned into a 17-yard touchdown pass from Dilfer (23-for-38, 209 yards) to Arnez Battle after an 81-yard San Francisco drive. But that drive accounted for 30% of the 49ers' offense (267 yards) for the entire day.

The rest of the game was about the Giants' defense. The 49ers' next drive ended after one play — a fumbled handoff that was recovered by Umenyiora, which set up a 5-yard touchdown run by Jacobs that gave the Giants a 13-7 second-quarter lead. The next drive by the 49ers (2-4) ended after one play, too — an interception by Sam Madison. That turned into a 29-yard Lawrence Tynes field goal that put the Giants up 16-7.

The Giants put the game away on the 49ers' first series of the second half, after San Francisco had pushed all the way to the Giants' 15. On first down, Dilfer dropped back and Umenyiora blew right by left tackle Jonas Jennings and smashed into Dilfer's back. In one motion, Umenyiora flattened Dilfer, corraled the loose ball, popped up and took

Giants receiver Amani Toomer catches a 4-yard touchdown pass in the first quarter.
Michael Appleton/Daily News

off for a 75-yard touchdown, giving the Giants an insurmountable 26-7 lead.

"That's a demonstration of the kind of talent he has," said linebacker Antonio Pierce.

"He made it look simple," Tom Coughlin added. "But it's not."

The Giants weren't done. They had time to convert an interception by Pierce into a 2-yard touchdown pass from Manning to Jeremy Shockey. Big plays like that have happened for the Giants' defense a lot during their five-game winning streak, in large part because they've had 25 sacks

"[UMENYIORA] MADE IT LOOK SIMPLE. BUT IT'S NOT."
—TOM COUGHLIN

in those games. That pressure has opened the floodgates on forced turnovers, including three fumbles and eight interceptions.

"We're stopping the run right now," said defensive end Justin Tuck, after the Giants held 49ers running back Frank Gore to 88 yards (though he did rush for 6.4 yards per carry). "You make a team one-dimensional and you can pretty much predict what they're going to do. And with the talent we've got on that defensive line, if we can figure out when they're going to pass, I don't think there's anybody that can stop us."

The 49ers, running the NFL's worst offense and with a backup quarterback, certainly didn't have much of a chance. It was so bad near the end, before the 49ers scored a garbage-time touchdown with 16 seconds remaining, that Mike Nolan considered pulling Dilfer and putting in Alex Smith, who hasn't played since injuring his shoulder.

"It just crossed my mind, because (Dilfer) was getting hit," Nolan said. "But I didn't want the other guy to get hit as well."

"I believe he was tired of getting hit," added Pierce. "Whether it was late, legal or illegal. He was tired of getting hit."

Consider that a not-so-subtle warning to Cleo Lemon, quarterback of the winless Miami Dolphins whom the Giants face in London next week, and every other quarterback they'll see during the second half of the season.

"At this point we're probably in some quarterbacks' heads," Michael Strahan said. "We want to continue to get the pressure to let them know what they're thinking was warranted."

Jeremy Shockey flips a football into the stands following his fourth-quarter TD.
Michael Appleton/Daily News

WEEK 7

	1st	2nd	3rd	4th	Final
49ERS	0	7	2	6	15
GIANTS	6	13	7	7	33

Scoring Summary

1st
GIANTS   Amani Toomer, 4 yd pass from Eli Manning kick failed, 7:47. Drive: 13 plays, 83 yards in 7:13.

2nd
49ERS   Arnaz Battle, 17 yd pass from Trent Dilfer (Joe Nedney kick is good), 9:50. Drive: 11 plays, 81 yards in 6:25.
GIANTS   Brandon Jacobs, 5 yd run (Lawrence Tynes kick is good), 6:15. Drive: 4 plays, 27 yards in 1:12.
GIANTS   Lawrence Tynes, 29 yd field goal, 2:50. Drive: 6 plays, 19 yards in 3:09.
GIANTS   Lawrence Tynes, 39 yd field goal, 0:17. Drive: 9 plays, 68 yards in 1:18.

3rd
GIANTS   Osi Umenyiora, 75 yd fumble (Lawrence Tynes kick is good), 12:53.
49ERS   Punt blocked by M.Norris out of bounds in end zone for a safety, 09:01.

4TH
GIANTS   Jeremy Shockey, 2 yd pass from Eli Manning (Lawrence Tynes kick is good), 10:50. Drive: 4 plays, 5 yards in 2:25.
49ERS   Darrell Jackson, 1 yd pass from Trent Dilfer pass failed, 0:16. Drive: 10 plays, 53 yards in 3:00.

Team Stats

	49ERS	GIANTS
1st Downs	20	21
3rd-Down Conversions	4-13	7-13
4th-Down Conversions	2-2	0-0
Punts-Average	5-52.6	4-28.0
Punts-Returns	2-4	3-16
Kickoffs-Returns	8-172	2-39
Interceptions-Returns	1-4	2-34
Penalties-Yards	13-82	8-67
Fumbles-Lost	3-2	0-0
Time of Possession	28:42	31:18
Total Net Yards	267	279
Total Plays	62	64
Net Yards Rushing	103	140
Rushes	18	31
Net Yards Passing	164	139
Comp.-Att.-Int.	23-38-2	18-32-1
Sacked-Yards Lost	6-45	1-7
Red Zone Efficiency	2/3-66%	3/4-75%

On a rainy day in London, Giants running back Brandon Jacobs led New York with 131 rushing yards.
AP Images

GIANTS BEAT DOLPHINS IN LONDON

October 29, 2007 ◆ By Ralph Vacchiano, Daily News

EVERY TIME ANOTHER wet football slipped out of Eli Manning's hands or another receiver slid on the muddy turf, another teammate would come up to Brandon Jacobs with the same message.

"The guys kept telling me, 'We've got to run, we've got to run,'" Jacobs said. "It was kind of tough throwing the ball around. We did the best that we can do on that field. But running the ball, that's what you do on a wet field."

As usual, the Giants did it in powerful fashion yesterday, riding Jacobs' career-high 131 yards to become the first NFL team to win a regular-season game outside of North America. They beat the winless Miami Dolphins, 13-10, in front of 81,176 fans at a wet, muddy and chilly Wembley Stadium, giving the Giants their first six-game winning streak in 13 years.

It was a historic win, even if it wasn't the best advertisement for American football. Thanks to typical England weather, including a driving morning rain, the converted soccer field already was torn up during warm-ups. When the driving rain started again in the second quarter, the conditions made the game a mess.

It wreaked havoc on the Giants' passing game. Manning completed just eight of 22 throws for 59 yards — his lowest total since Dec. 12, 2004, the infamous game in Baltimore during his rookie season when he went 4-for-18 for 27 yards. Things were so bad for him that early in the fourth quarter he had as many rushing yards (28) as passing yards.

"When it was raining hard at some times, the ball was slick," Manning said. "With the conditions, we weren't throwing it especially well."

"The weather certainly affected us," Amani Toomer added. "Our offense could not do as much as we wanted to do."

That was evident on the Giants' first drive, when Manning drove them to the Miami 3-yard line. But he ended it by overthrowing two wide-open receivers — Toomer and fullback Madison Hedgecock — in the end zone on successive plays.

On the bright side, that allowed Lawrence Tynes, a native of Greenock, Scotland, to fittingly score the first points in the NFL's first regular-season game overseas. His 30-yard field goal with 3:33 left in the first quarter gave the Giants a 3-0 lead.

That's when the rain really started coming down, and the field started coming up in clumps on the players' spikes. But it didn't seem to affect Jacobs, who, with his white uniform covered in mud, rushed 11 times for 66 yards in the first half.

"(The conditions) kind of hindered some things," Jacobs said. "Instead of running for whatever I ran for, it could've been about 75 more (yards) added to that. There were a lot of (holes) I saw out there that I wasn't able to get to because of the traction."

Regardless, he ran for enough, and so did Manning, who joined the rush with 59 seconds left in the first half when, after seeing no one open to his right, he took off to the left for a 10-yard touchdown run. That put the Giants up 10-0.

The Giants made it 13-0 just 57 seconds later when they turned a fumble by Miami quarterback Cleo Lemon into a 41-yard Tynes field goal.

Dolphins kicker Jay Feely, the ex-Giant who missed a 48-yard field goal on the opening series, kicked a 29-yarder near the end of the third quarter to pull the Dolphins (0-8) within 13-3. And that's when things really became interesting.

First, Tynes missed a 29-yard field goal on the next series — a mistake that Tom Coughlin said "would have been very regrettable had the

Dolphins come back on us." More regrettable was the Giants' next possession, which featured four penalties in a five-play sequence that sent them from a first-and-10 on the Dolphins' 34 all the way back to a second-and-37 on their own 39.

After they punted the ball away, the Dolphins made them pay when Lemon (17-for-30, 149 yards) threw a 21-yard touchdown pass to Ted Ginn Jr. to pull the Dolphins within three points with 1:54 to play.

"We thought we were in pretty good shape defensively for a long time," Coughlin said. "Nevertheless, that last drive, the ability to score under those situations, was a shocker to me."

The Giants managed to escape only after Feely's onside kickoff went out of bounds. The Giants took a knee on their final three plays, a tactic that drew loud boos from the otherwise cheery British crowd.

"I thought the fans were great and they certainly were loud," Coughlin said. "The only thing they didn't understand, quite frankly, is us kneeling on the ball at the end. I guess you'd have to know football to understand that."

The Giants understood that those "victory" plays meant they had avoided what surely would have been the longest and most agonizing flight of their career. Instead, they can enjoy their seven-hour trip back home this afternoon at 6-2 for the second consecutive season.

And now that they are done being the NFL's goodwill ambassadors, they can focus on making sure this year's first-half success turns out better than it did a year ago, when they went 2-6 to finish at 8-8.

"We still have a long ways to go," said cornerback Sam Madison. "But it's a totally different feeling from last year."

WEEK 8

	1st	2nd	3rd	4th	Final
DOLPHINS	0	0	3	7	10
GIANTS	3	10	0	0	13

Scoring Summary

1st
GIANTS — Lawrence Tynes, 20 yd field goal, 3:33. Drive: 11 plays, 59 yards in 4:47.

2nd
GIANTS — Eli Manning, 10 yd run (Lawrence Tynes kick is good), 0:59. Drive: 14 plays, 69 yards in 8:07.

GIANTS — Lawrence Tynes, 41 yd field goal, 0:02. Drive: 4 plays, 11 yards in 0:24.

3rd
DOLPHINS — Jay Feely, 29 yd field goal, 1:04. Drive: 8 plays, 40 yards in 4:12.

4TH
DOLPHINS — Ted Ginn, 21 yd pass from Cleo Lemon (Jay Feely kick is good), 1:54. Drive: 12 plays, 80 yards in 2:11.

Team Stats

	DOLPHINS	GIANTS
1st Downs	18	19
3rd-Down Conversions	6-13	3-11
4th-Down Conversions	0-0	1-1
Punts-Average	4-43.3	4-41.8
Punts-Returns	0-0	3-35
Kickoffs-Returns	4-74	2-66
Interceptions-Returns	0-0	0-0
Penalties-Yards	7-61	7-60
Fumbles-Lost	3-2	3-1
Time of Possession	27:55	32:05
Total Net Yards	245	238
Total Plays	59	60
Net Yards Rushing	126	189
Rushes	26	37
Net Yards Passing	119	49
Comp.-Att.-Int.	17-30-0	8-22-0
Sacked-Yards Lost	3-30	1-10
Red Zone Efficiency	1/2-50%	1/3-33%

A pair of Miami defenders struggle to tackle R.W. McQuarters. *AP Images*

Brandon Jacobs finished with 95 rushing yards against the Cowboys. His game-tying TD run in the fourth quarter was called back due to a penalty. *Michael Appleton/Daily News*

OWENS, ROMO LEAD COWBOYS PAST GIANTS

November 12, 2007 ◆ By Ralph Vacchiano, Daily News

THEIR HOPES OF a division title have been all but dashed, their playoff picture has been muddied and for a third straight year, given a chance to prove they were the best team in the NFC, the Giants proved only that they weren't.

Of course, none of those facts has shaken their confidence. And nothing that happened in their 31-20 loss to Dallas yesterday at the Meadowlands was enough to make the Giants concede the Cowboys are the better team.

"They're absolutely not a better team than us," said defensive end Osi Umenyiora. "They may have played better today in the second half, but I'd never say they were a better team."

Maybe the Giants won't say it, but almost everyone else will be thinking it after the Cowboys (8-1) completed a two-game sweep of the Giants (6-3), snapped their six-game winning streak, and opened up a three-game lead (two, plus the tiebreaker) in the NFC East with seven games to go. Cowboys quarterback Tony Romo again shredded the Giants, tossing four touchdowns passes against them for the second time this season.

That included a 50-yarder to a wide-open Terrell Owens (6 catches, 125 yards) that sealed the game with 10:43 to go.

The Giants, though, chose to look past the fact that the Cowboys lit them up for 76 points and 801 yards in two games, and focused on how they felt they blew the game with their own unforced errors. The biggest two may have come in the second half, just after Romo (20-for-28, 247 yards) and Owens hooked up for a 25-yard touchdown that put the Cowboys up 24-17.

On the ensuing kickoff, rookie Ahmad Bradshaw returned it all the way to the Dallas 2. But a holding penalty on rookie tight end Kevin Boss — away from the play — brought the ball back to the Giants' 17. Later that drive, Brandon Jacobs appeared to score a game-tying touchdown on a 6-yard run, only to see it called back on a debated hold call on guard Chris Snee.

Both Giants disputed the penalties on the drive, but the damage was done. The Giants, who wore their red uniforms, had to settle for a 26-yard Lawrence Tynes field goal that closed their deficit to 24-20. Five plays later, the Romo-to-Owens 50-yarder put the game away.

"We were our own worst enemy," said Tom Coughlin. "We have no excuses."

The Giants' penalties (eight in all, including three delay of game calls on the offense) weren't the only mistakes. On the Cowboys' first drive, receiver Tony Curtis was left wide open in the end zone, about half a field away from Giants safety James Butler, and caught a 15-yard touchdown pass.

Rookie corner Aaron Ross had Cowboys receiver Patrick Crayton wrapped up late in the first half, but let him escape for a 20-yard touchdown and a

Jeremy Shockey flexes after scoring on an 8-yard pass from Eli Manning in the first quarter.
Lee Weissman/Daily News

17-14 Cowboys lead. And rookie safety Michael Johnson missed a key third-down tackle on Cowboys running back Marion Barber one play before the final Romo-to-Owens touchdown pass.

And perhaps most damaging to the offense, after giving up only nine sacks in the first eight games of the season, the Giants allowed Eli Manning (23-of-34, 236 yards) to be sacked five times. That kept them out of sync all game, despite a career day from tight end Jeremy Shockey (12 catches, 129 yards).

"We made a lot of foolish errors," Coughlin said, before cutting his postgame press conference short. "I'm not going to get into it, but the rookie errors stand out. We made some real critical errors there and if guys are going to play they have the responsibility to play well."

Still, despite the blunders, the game was tied 17-17 at the half.

"We felt like we were right there," said safety Gibril Wilson. "Hopefully we get to see them again."

The Cowboys probably would like that too,

especially after the way they broke out their big-play offense in the second half. It was a reminder, as Cowboys coach Wade Phillips said, that "we don't have a good offense. We have a great offense."

It wasn't easy to find Giants who agreed, even though their vaunted pass rush only sacked Romo twice and their secondary was exposed just like it was in a 45-35 loss on opening night in Dallas.

"We made some mistakes, but you can't tell me we're not a good enough team to win that game," added Michael Strahan. "That's a good sign."

Despite a mountain of evidence and seemingly insurmountable odds, the Giants are not ready to concede the NFC East.

"It does put us behind the eight ball, and if you have ever played pool, I have seen people make shots from behind the eight ball," said defensive end Justin Tuck. "We aren't looking at (the division) as out of reach. We just put ourselves in a bad position."

Tom Coughlin reacts to a call during the Giants'
Week 10 game against the Cowboys.
Michael Appleton/Daily News

WEEK 10

	1st	2nd	3rd	4th	Final
COWBOYS	7	10	7	7	31
GIANTS	7	10	0	3	20

Scoring Summary

1st
COWBOYS Tony Curtis, 15 yd pass from Tony Romo (Nick Folk kick is good), 11:10. Drive: 7 plays, 65 yards in 3:50.
GIANTS Jeremy Shockey, 8 yd pass from Eli Manning (Lawrence Tynes kick is good), 6:13. Drive: 8 plays, 67 yards in 4:57.

2nd
COWBOYS Nick Folk, 44 yd field goal, 14:56. Drive: 6 plays, 13 yards in 2:56.
GIANTS Reuben Droughns, 1 yd run (Lawrence Tynes kick is good), 4:33. Drive: 11 plays, 60 yards in 7:22.
COWBOYS Patrick Crayton, 20 yd pass from Tony Romo (Nick Folk kick is good), 0:27. Drive: 7 plays, 68 yards in 1:21.
GIANTS Lawrence Tynes, 40 yd field goal, 0:01. Drive: 2 plays, 44 yards in 0:26.

3rd
COWBOYS Terrell Owens, 25 yd pass from Tony Romo (Nick Folk kick is good), 7:14. Drive: 12 plays, 86 yards in 6:27.

4TH
GIANTS Lawrence Tynes, 26 yd field goal, 13:18. Drive: 16 plays, 75 yards in 8:56.
COWBOYS Terrell Owens, 50 yd pass from Tony Romo (Nick Folk kick is good), 10:43. Drive: 5 plays, 70 yards in 2:35.

Team Stats

	COWBOYS	GIANTS
1st Downs	19	23
3rd-Down Conversions	5-11	7-14
4th-Down Conversions	0-0	0-1
Punts-Average	4-35.8	4-38.3
Punts-Returns	0-0	1-10
Kickoffs-Returns	4-86	6-79
Interceptions-Returns	2-26	1-0
Penalties-Yards	10-84	8-70
Fumbles-Lost	1-0	1-0
Time of Possession	25:12	34:48
Total Net Yards	323	300
Total Plays	54	67
Net Yards Rushing	80	106
Rushes	25	28
Net Yards Passing	243	194
Comp.-Att.-Int.	20-28-1	23-34-2
Sacked-Yards Lost	1-4	5-42
Red Zone Efficiency	1/2-50%	2/3-66%

Giants cornerback Sam Madison (29) celebrates after intercepting a Detroit pass late in the fourth quarter.
AP Images

GIANTS' DEFENSE TAMES LIONS

November 19, 2007 ◆ By Ralph Vacchiano, Daily News

MAYBE IT WASN'T as dramatic as the goal-line stand that turned the Giants' season around eight weeks ago, but in the end it was just as big. That's why everyone on the sidelines felt the same way when Sam Madison's late interception finally settled matters.

"Once we got that last ball," Madison said, "it was a sigh of relief."

The Giants were relieved with 48 seconds remaining as Madison's interception finally halted the Detroit Lions' late rally, but not just because it allowed them to escape noisy Ford Field with a 16-10 victory Sunday. It also gave them the bounce-back win they never managed to get last year in their miserable second half of the season.

So now, as far as the Giants (7-3) are concerned, they finally have put any talk of another second-half collapse away for good.

"We knew if we lost we'd hear all that again," said Osi Umenyiora. "We just couldn't have that."

They won't because they did what the 2006 team could never do — they put a little distance between themselves, the Lions (6-4) and the other wild-card contenders. And they did it with a defense that proved that the only fluky thing about it was its subpar performance against the Dallas Cowboys one week earlier, this time shutting down a Lions offense that was averaging 31 points per game at home.

Actually, the defense didn't completely contain Detroit. Jon Kitna threw for 377 yards (28-for-43) and he had two 100-yard receivers — Shaun McDonald (seven catches, 113 yards) and Roy Williams (6-106). But the Giants did stop the Detroit running game (25 yards) and forced four turnovers, including three interceptions.

Two of the thefts came deep inside their own territory in the final two minutes of the game.

"Those last three or four plays, two or three guys were hitting (Kitna) at a time, making him throw those balls up, and guys were getting those picks," said Michael Strahan, who led the pass rush with three sacks. "If you look at our past history, that's been one of our problems."

In fact, most of their past problems were on display in the fourth quarter. They already were decimated by injuries, having lost linebacker Mathias

> "WE KNEW IF WE LOST WE'D HEAR ALL THAT AGAIN. WE JUST COULDN'T HAVE THAT."
> —OSI UMENYIORA

Giants safety James Butler intercepts a pass intended for Lions receiver Shaun McDonald in the fourth quarter. *AP Images*

Kiwanuka (broken left fibia) probably for the season, and running back Brandon Jacobs (left hamstring) for at least the rest of the game. And their offense, which had done a decent job led by Eli Manning (28-for-39, 283 yards), was shutting down at the most inopportune time.

That gave the high-flying Lions a chance to finally take advantage of the Giants' porous secondary — one Williams said, "We were beating left and right, all day long," though never enough to get into the end zone. That changed with 4:24 remaining when rookie receiver Calvin Johnson out-jumped cornerback Kevin Dockery to catch a 35-yard touchdown pass that cut the Giants' lead to 16-10.

The Giants responded by going three-and-out, giving the Lions a chance to drive for the win with 2:25 remaining. And they were inches away from doing just that, but James Butler, the Giants' 6-3 safety, out-jumped McDonald, the Lions' 5-10 receiver, to intercept what would have been a 51-yard touchdown pass at the goal line with 1:54 to play.

But even that wasn't enough, because the Giants went three-and-out again, giving Kitna one more opportunity with 1:25 to play. It ended

WEEK 11

	1st	2nd	3rd	4th	Final
LIONS	0	0	3	7	10
GIANTS	3	7	3	3	16

Scoring Summary

1st
GIANTS Lawrence Tynes, 28 yd field goal, 0:37. Drive: 10 plays, 81 yards in 5:11.

2nd
GIANTS Brandon Jacobs, 10 yd pass from Eli Manning (Lawrence Tynes kick is good), 0:23. Drive: 11 plays, 80 yards in 3:44.

3rd
LIONS   Jason Hanson, 42 yd field goal, 10:52. Drive: 8 plays, 43 yards in 3:40.
GIANTS Lawrence Tynes, 46 yd field goal, 2:39. Drive: 6 plays, 30 yards in 3:18.

4TH
GIANTS Lawrence Tynes, 20 yd field goal, 11:15. Drive: 9 plays, 53 yards in 4:50.
LIONS   Calvin Johnson, 35 yd pass from Jon Kitna (Jason Hanson kick is good), 4:34. Drive: 4 plays, 82 yards in 1:18.

Team Stats

	LIONS	GIANTS
1st Downs	17	19
3rd-Down Conversions	1-10	4-14
4th-Down Conversions	0-0	0-0
Punts-Average	6-43.2	6-48.3
Punts-Returns	2-8	3-21
Kickoffs-Returns	4-79	2-97
Interceptions-Returns	0-0	3-3
Penalties-Yards	7-40	6-47
Fumbles-Lost	3-1	3-2
Time of Possession	24:43	35:17
Total Net Yards	376	341
Total Plays	57	68
Net Yards Rushing	25	72
Rushes	11	27
Net Yards Passing	351	269
Comp.-Att.-Int.	28-43-3	28-39-0
Sacked-Yards Lost	3-26	2-14
Red Zone Efficiency	0/0-0%	1/3-33%

when Kitna's last pass went off McDonald's fingertips and was corralled by Madison at the Giants' 31.

"I think I actually said, 'Thank you, Sam,' as I ran on the field," said center Shaun O'Hara. "I personally thanked him for allowing us to get out of here with a win."

"We should have been able to run that clock out," guard Chris Snee added. "We didn't do our job."

The offense did enough of its job, but hurt itself with a couple of key fumbles in Lions territory — one by receiver Sinorice Moss in the second quarter and one by Jacobs (11 carries, 54 yards) in the third. They also stumbled in the red zone, scoring only once, on Jacobs' 10-yard TD reception, in three trips inside the Lions' 20. They were bailed out by three Lawrence Tynes field goals (28, 46, 20) that helped them build a 10-0 lead that eventually became 16-3.

The rest was up to a defense that was intent on proving it was for real.

"Absolutely," said defensive end Justin Tuck. "Sometimes this defense can be a bend-but-don't break, and sometimes this defense can be out-right dominating. For the most part, I thought our defense did a good job of pretty much dominating the football game."

As a result, the Giants bounced back from last week's disappointing loss against the Cowboys. And once and for all, they hope this is the win that proves to everyone this isn't last season.

"You hear all week long about how you're going to collapse, lose eight in a row and all that stuff," Snee said. "But I've been saying the whole time, this is a different team."

Giants running back Brandon Jacobs led New York with 54 rushing yards, 49 receiving yards and the team's lone touchdown. *AP Images*

Eli Manning reacts after being sacked by the Vikings in the second half. *Michael Appleton/Daily News*

TOUGH DAY FOR ELI AGAINST VIKINGS

November 26, 2007 ◆ By Ralph Vacchiano, Daily News

IT DIDN'T MATTER that the Giants could remember their past failures against the Minnesota Vikings. Eli Manning condemned them to repeat them.

In a shocking, yet eerily familiar performance Sunday, Manning threw four interceptions, including a team-record three that were returned for touchdowns, as the Giants (7-4) inexcusably lost, 41-17, to the Vikings (5-6) at the Meadowlands. It was an even worse performance than Manning's four-interception game against Minnesota two years ago and it came with brother Peyton looking on from a luxury box.

"I did not, in my worst moment, think I'd be standing here talking about history repeating itself," Tom Coughlin said. "But it did."

Nobody could have seen this disaster coming — not even after Vikings quarterback Tavaris Jackson hit Sidney Rice with a 60-yard touchdown pass on the third play of the game. The Giants rebounded from that, scoring on a 1-yard run by Reuben Droughns on the ensuing possession — a drive in which Manning was 3-for-3 for 45 yards.

That was a pretty good start but the dreadful end was in sight.

The deluge started when Darren Sharper — who made three interceptions in Minnesota's 24-21 win over the Giants in 2005 — returned a pick 20 yards for a touchdown in the first quarter. Two drives later, an interception by safety Dwight Smith set up

an 8-yard touchdown run by Chester Taylor.

Manning (21-for-49, 273 yards, one touchdown) would add two more interceptions in the fourth quarter — one that Smith returned 93 yards for a touchdown, and another that linebacker Chad Greenway ran back 37 yards for a score.

No NFL defense had returned three interceptions for touchdowns since the Seattle Seahawks did it against the Kansas City Chiefs way back in 1984.

"I wish there was some simple explanation for this game, but there isn't," Coughlin said. "We played very, very poorly. In the National Football League, you obviously cannot wrap it up and hand it to the guy across the field. And we did."

Added tight end Jeremy Shockey: "If we play like that we're not going to win against a high school team."

Manning explained his personal horror show against the NFL's 31st-ranked passing defense — and one that was missing its top corner, Antoine Winfield — by saying simply that the Vikings "just had a good plan." Eventually he conceded that "I didn't play well."

In fact, he was so ineffective that Coughlin considered benching him in the fourth quarter, but he preferred to send a message to his beaten team that "we weren't giving up.

"I just don't like that feeling (of pulling the quarterback)," Coughlin said. "I wasn't going to

Giants wide receiver Amani Toomer finished the game with 83 receiving yards on four catches.
Lee Weissman/Daily News

do that to him and I wasn't going to do that to me and us."

"If we had 11 players that could've gone in for the 11 starters," added center Shaun O'Hara, "then he should've pulled us all."

The Giants may not have given up — they even added a garbage-time, 6-yard touchdown pass from Manning to Plaxico Burress (seven catches, 93 yards) with 5:54 to play — but the fans certainly did. They made a mad dash for the exits after Smith's big return made the score 34-10 with just under 14 minutes remaining. Not surprisingly, those who were left in the crowd booed every ensuing series when Coughlin kept sending Manning back onto the field.

And it was no wonder. The offensive line's play forced Manning to be on the run for most of the afternoon, and even when he did have time something was out of sync.

"When you throw four interceptions it is never

a good day," Manning said. "Every one has its own story."

None of those tales was good. The first one, by Sharper that made it 14-7, was the result of a miscommunication between Manning and Shockey, when the quarterback misread a blitz and the tight end didn't stop his route. The second, a Smith interception that led to the Taylor touchdown, appeared to result from a similar mixup between Manning and Burress. The third chapter, also by Smith, was tipped by Vikings defensive end Ray Edwards. And the fourth, which made the score 41-10 with 12:59 remaining, came when Greenway just jumped Shockey's route.

Add it all up and it became what O'Hara called "an ugly, ugly, ugly loss. I don't know if you can use enough 'uglies.'" And it was shocking, coming one week after the Giants won in Detroit to seemingly establish themselves as the third-best

Giants running back Reuben Droughns collected 46 of New York's 75 rushing yards.
Michael Appleton/Daily News

team in the NFC.

"I don't know if I'd use the word 'shocked,'" guard Chris Snee said. "I'd use the word 'embarrassed.'"

"In a lot of ways," added Michael Strahan, "you have to look at it as almost comical."

But there's nothing funny about the fact the Giants were pulled a little closer back to the pack in the NFC wild-card chase, with their two-game cushion cut in half with five games remaining.

"We always do this," Shockey said. "We always make it hard on ourselves. What can I say? This is what we do."

WEEK 12

	1st	2nd	3rd	4th	Final
VIKINGS	14	10	3	14	41
GIANTS	7	0	3	7	17

Scoring Summary

1st
VIKINGS — Sidney Rice, 60 yd pass from Tarvaris Jackson (Ryan Longwell kick is good), 14:19. Drive: 2 plays, 60 yards in 0:41.
GIANTS — Reuben Droughns, 1 yd run (Lawrence Tynes kick is good), 9:25. Drive: 8 plays, 65 yards in 4:54.
VIKINGS — Darren Sharper, 20 yd interception return (Ryan Longwell kick is good), 3:15.

2nd
VIKINGS — Chester Taylor, 8 yd run (Ryan Longwell kick is good), 9:49. Drive: 1 plays, 8 yards in 0:09.
VIKINGS — Ryan Longwell, 46 yd field goal, 3:16. Drive: 9 plays, 37 yards in 4:47.

3rd
GIANTS — Lawrence Tynes, 48 yd field goal, 11:07. Drive: 10 plays, 48 yards in 3:53.
VIKINGS — Ryan Longwell, 26 yd field goal, 1:43. Drive: 14 plays, 69 yards in 9:24.

4TH
VIKINGS — Dwight Smith, 93 yd interception return (Ryan Longwell kick is good), 13:41.
VIKINGS — Chad Greenway, 37 yd interception return (Ryan Longwell kick is good), 12:59.
GIANTS — Plaxico Burress, 6 yd pass from Eli Manning (Lawrence Tynes kick is good), 5:54. Drive: 7 plays, 44 yards in 2:51.

Team Stats

	VIKINGS	GIANTS
1st Downs	15	18
3rd-Down Conversions	5-13	7-17
4th-Down Conversions	1-1	0-2
Punts-Average	5-40.6	4-46.3
Punts-Returns	0-0	2-12
Kickoffs-Returns	3-66	8-176
Interceptions-Returns	4-169	0-0
Penalties-Yards	4-15	5-30
Fumbles-Lost	1-0	0-0
Time of Possession	32:14	27:46
Total Net Yards	251	309
Total Plays	55	71
Net Yards Rushing	127	75
Rushes	39	19
Net Yards Passing	124	234
Comp.-Att.-Int.	10-12-0	21-49-4
Sacked-Yards Lost	4-5	3-39
Red Zone Efficiency	1/3-33%	2/3-66%

Giants quarterback Eli Manning rebounded from a pair of interceptions to lead the Giants' 14-point turn-around in the fourth quarter. *AP Images*

MANNING LEADS COMEBACK VICTORY

December 3, 2007 ◆ By Ralph Vacchiano, Daily News

HERE WERE CHEERS and screams of joy coming out of the Giants' locker room Sunday night, the sounds of a team that had just saved its season. And out of the celebration emerged their embattled quarterback, who had just endured a Hell Week.

Moments earlier, Eli Manning had dispersed the angry mob that was ready to run him out of town by leading the Giants to two unanswered touchdowns in the final seven minutes. He had rebounded from two interceptions and a fumble to put together a perfect final drive that gave the Giants a shocking 21-16 win over the Chicago Bears.

Then he stepped to the podium in the same calm, cool, unaffected way that had enraged so many one week earlier.

"Well," Manning said when asked how redemption feels, "it's nice."

That was the understatement of the day after the Giants' comeback win. They trailed for most of the day, but when Reuben Droughns — playing for Derrick Ward, who left the game with a broken leg — rumbled into the end zone from two yards out with 1:33 remaining, it capped a stunning turn of events. The Giants (8-4) were down 16-7 before Manning led them to two touchdowns in the final 6:54.

In his 51st career start, it was the seventh time he's rallied the Giants to a win in the fourth quarter.

"That just tells you the mentality of that guy," said linebacker Antonio Pierce. "All the critics and hell is coming down on him. He could have easily flopped over, put his head down and put the game away. But he didn't. He came back and made some of the biggest plays of the game."

"He kept the same demeanor," said guard Chris Snee. "He wasn't rattled or skittish, which I believe was the term being thrown around. He was confident."

Manning's composure was obvious in the fourth quarter, when the Giants got the ball with 11:45 remaining trailing 16-7. Two drives earlier, Manning had blown a huge chance when, from the Bears' 1, he spun out of the hands of Bears defensive end Alex Brown and tried to float a pass to Plaxico Burress in the corner of the end zone.

When he threw it short and it was picked off by Charles Tillman, the Giants appeared done.

But not Manning. He went 3-for-5 for 33 yards on their next-to-last drive and even shook off the loss of Ward to hit Amani Toomer (six catches, 69 yards) in the end zone. It was a bad, low pass that was first ruled incomplete, but the Giants challenged and the referee overturned it, ruling it a 6-yard touchdown catch.

That pulled the Giants within 16-14, and they weren't done. After the Giants sacked Rex Grossman for the sixth time, forcing a three-and-

Amani Toomer signals to Giants head coach Tom Coughlin that his fourth-quarter TD catch was good. *AP Images*

WEEK 13

	1st	2nd	3rd	4th	Final
BEARS	7	6	3	0	16
GIANTS	0	7	0	14	21

Scoring Summary

1st Quarter
BEARS   Desmond Clark, 1 yd pass from Rex Grossman (Robbie Gould kick is good), 9:58. Drive: 9 plays, 79 yards in 3:08.

2nd Quarter
GIANTS   Derrick Ward, 2 yd run (Lawrence Tynes kick is good), 10:25. Drive: 4 plays, 32 yards in 1:40.
BEARS   Robbie Gould, 35 yd field goal, 4:38. Drive: 8 plays, 54 yards in 3:13.
BEARS   Robbie Gould, 46 yd field goal, 0:00. Drive: 14 plays, 62 yards in 2:53.

3rd Quarter
BEARS   Robbie Gould, 41 yd field goal, 10:52. Drive: 7 plays, 2 yards in 3:04.

4th Quarter
GIANTS   Amani Toomer, 6 yd pass from Eli Manning (Lawrence Tynes kick is good), 6:54. Drive: 11 plays, 75 yards in 4:51.
GIANTS   Reuben Droughns, 2 yd run (Lawrence Tynes kick is good), 1:33. Drive: 9 plays, 77 yards in 3:22.

Team Stats

	BEARS	GIANTS
1st Downs	18	24
3rd-Down Conversions	6-19	5-12
4th-Down Conversions	1-1	1-1
Punts-Average	8-39.5	5-40.8
Punts-Returns	3-16	5-32
Kickoffs-Returns	2-29	4-72
Interceptions-Returns	2-1	0-0
Penalties-Yards	10-71	2-10
Fumbles-Lost	0-0	4-2
Time of Possession	29:24	30:36
Total Net Yards	312	356
Total Plays	75	66
Net Yards Rushing	68	175
Rushes	23	37
Net Yards Passing	244	181
Comp.-Att.-Int.	25-46-0	16-27-2
Sacked-Yards Lost	6-52	2-14
Red Zone Efficiency	1/4-25%	3/4-75%

out, Manning (16-for-27, 195 yards) got the ball and the game back in his hands at the Giants' 23 with 4:55 remaining.

He wasted little time, going 4-for-4 for 62 yards on Big Blue's final drive, including a gutsy, 15-yard pass that Burress caught at the 2-yard line, setting up Droughns' game-winning touchdown. Then the Giants survived three Grossman passes to the end zone from 28 yards away to make Manning's comeback stick.

"It wasn't the prettiest," Manning said. "At times it was flat-out ugly. But it was sweet."

It definitely wasn't pretty. One week after a four-interception performance in a 41-17 loss to Minnesota, Manning threw his first interception yesterday on the fourth play of the game. That looked even worse when Grossman (25-for-46, 296 yards) completed his first eight passes and ripped through the Giants using a no-huddle

offense for an easy touchdown on Chicago's first drive.

Manning and the Giants did rebound nicely, as Ward — in the midst of a career-best, 154-yard performance — set up his own 2-yard touchdown with a 31-yard run. But Manning fumbled on the next drive, leading to a Bears field goal that put Chicago (5-7) up 10-7. And Ward fumbled early in the third quarter, leading to the field goal that gave the Bears a 16-7 lead.

What came next, though was, in the words of Tom Coughlin, "really a win that I think will give our team some inspiration."

The comeback allowed the Giants to at least temporarily prevent the Dallas Cowboys (11-1)

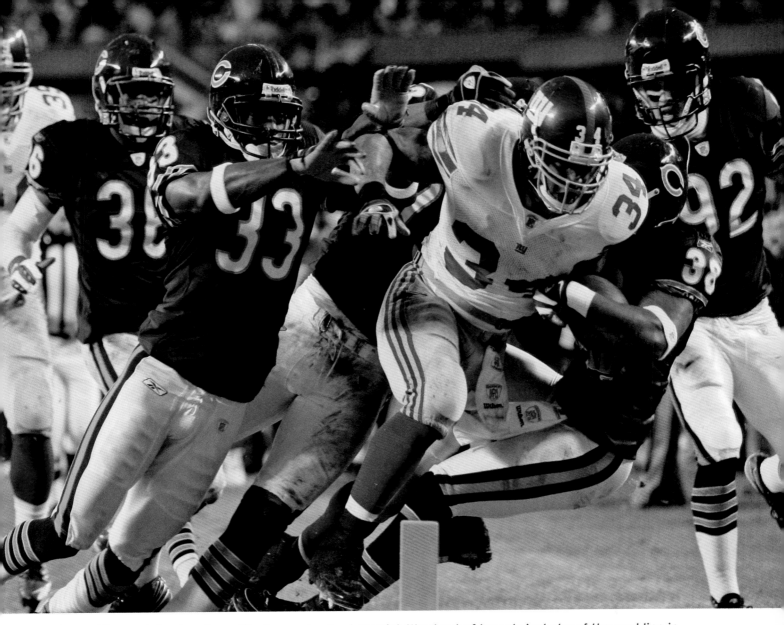

Several Bears defenders force Giants running back Derrick Ward out of bounds just shy of the goal line in the second quarter. *AP Images*

from clinching the NFC East and maintain a two-game lead in the NFC wild-card chase.

Maybe more importantly, it was an enormous boost to a roomful of egos that were understandably beginning to sag.

"Really, (being) 8-4 is huge," Toomer said. "I think it's huge for our psyche. Hopefully we can use this win as a springboard, get some confidence and keep going into the playoffs."

The playoffs aren't assured, but it certainly feels that way to the Giants. They believe they've got the team to get there and do some damage.

In Manning, they're sure they've got the quarterback, too.

"That's the Eli Manning we knew," said center Shaun O'Hara. "You can't take one bad game and stamp it on somebody's chest."

"The significant way in which he played down the stretch," Coughlin added, "makes a strong statement about him."

Eagles kicker David Akers, left, reacts after missing a 57-yard field goal attempt in the closing seconds.
AP Images

GIANTS KICK EAGLES ASIDE

December 10, 2007 ◆ By Ralph Vacchiano, Daily News

THE GIANTS HAD COME FROM behind on the road for the second straight week, and once again were barely hanging on. They felt good, though, when the Eagles' David Akers trotted out to attempt a potential game-tying 57-yard field goal.

Brandon Jacobs thought, "He had no shot whatsoever." Many of his Giants teammates felt the same ... until they looked up and watched the kick.

It was long enough and was straight enough to give the Giants a few more breathless seconds, but in the end it hooked just enough to give them a huge sigh of relief. And when Akers' shot bounced off the right goalpost and harmlessly away with one second remaining, the Giants were able to celebrate their escape from Philly with a 16-13 victory.

"I was holding my breath, man," Michael Strahan said. "I'm glad that goalpost was right where it was — not an inch left or right."

"That," added defensive end Justin Tuck, "took three years off my life."

The victory did wonders for the Giants even though a few moments later the Dallas Cowboys would officially clinch the NFC East with a come-from-behind win in Detroit. The triumph not only assured the Giants (9-4) of a winning season, but it also made their third consecutive playoff berth inevitable. In fact, they can clinch it with a win at home against Washington on Sunday night.

And after the way they have won the last two weeks, the Giants certainly can say they're battle-tested heading toward the playoffs. Last week in Chicago, they needed to rally from nine points down late in the fourth quarter. This time they needed to overcome themselves.

The Giants' biggest problem was committing turnovers — specifically two second-half fumbles by Jacobs. That explains why the running back said, "I was one of the happiest guys on the sidelines," when Akers missed. Returning after a two-game absence due to a hamstring injury that hasn't fully healed, Jacobs fumbled on the third play of the second half, setting up Philly at the Giants' 8, and again at the Eagles' 10 with 5:51 left in the game.

Jacobs disputed the first call, which came on a screen pass ("I didn't catch the ball," he said), but it didn't matter because both times the Giants'

> "I WAS HOLDING MY BREATH. I'M GLAD THAT GOALPOST WAS RIGHT WHERE IT WAS . . ."
> —MICHAEL STRAHAN

defense responded. After the first fumble, the defense pushed the Eagles (5-8) backward and forced them to settle for a 29-yard field goal and a 10-6 lead.

"That was huge," Tom Coughlin said. "You talk about a tremendous momentum shift."

After the second fumble, the Eagles did push across midfield. But on fourth-and-6 from the Giants' 44, linebacker Antonio Pierce — who was nursing a sprained ankle that many of his teammates said should have kept him out of the game — hit receiver Jason Avant just enough to force him to drop Donovan McNabb's pass.

"That's probably the play of the game," Tuck said. "We expect that from him. He's our Superman."

Of course, it's possible Superman may have hit his target a little early, and that the officials missed the pass interference call.

"I really don't care," Pierce said. "It didn't get called. It's irrelevant. It's one of those plays like Franco Harris' catch (the Immaculate Reception). Did he catch it or not? We got the win, and that's all that matters."

The credit for that goes to a banged-up defense that limited the damage the Eagles inflicted. McNabb was an efficient 20-for-30 for 179 yards and was sacked only three times — nine fewer than the last time he played the Giants — but he never was able to take advantage of an all-rookie safety corps of Michael Johnson and Craig Dahl.

In fact, the Eagles' only play over 20 yards was a 21-yard run by Brian Westbrook (116 yards rushing, 38 yards receiving). After the way Philly sliced through the Giants on the opening drive and scored on an easy 18-yard pass to Westbrook, that was a bit of a surprise.

"They had the blitzkrieg going in the first series," Coughlin said. "We were reeling, but we settled down."

And though it took awhile for the Giants' offense to get in gear, it eventually did. The always gimpy Plaxico Burress caught seven passes for 136 yards — his fourth 100-yard receiving day in seven games against the Eagles as a Giant. That included a 20-yard touchdown catch that

gave the Giants the lead for good, 13-10 with 5:59 left in the third quarter, and a 41-yarder on the next drive that set up a 23-yard Lawrence Tynes field goal.

Actually, Burress' day could have been bigger since Manning overthrew him when he was open in the end zone on third-and-goal from the 4, just before Tynes kicked the field goal. Missed opportunities like that, and Jacobs' fumble at the 10 late in the fourth quarter were very nearly the story of the game.

That's the way it looked as Akers' kick sailed toward the goalposts.

"They got close," Tuck said. "But they didn't get there."

Added Jacobs: "Thank goodness for that goalpost."

WEEK 14

	1st	2nd	3rd	4th	Final
EAGLES	7	0	3	3	13
GIANTS	0	6	10	0	16

Scoring Summary

1st
EAGLES Brian Westbrook, 18 yd pass from Donovan McNabb (David Akers kick is good), 11:47. Drive: 6 plays, 68 yards in 3:13.
2nd
GIANTS Lawrence Tynes, 19 yd field goal, 11:06. Drive: 13 plays, 84 yards in 6:25.
GIANTS Lawrence Tynes, 23 yd field goa , 0:00. Drive: 9 plays, 45 yards in 1:23.
3rd
EAGLES David Akers, 29 yd field goal, 12:42.
GIANTS Plaxico Burress, 20 yd pass from Eli Manning (Lawrence Tynes kick is good), 5:59. Drive: 3 plays, 37 yards in 1:11.
GIANTS Lawrence Tynes, 23 yd field goal, 0:48. Drive: 7 plays, 61 yards in 3:06.
4TH
EAGLES David Akers, 39 yd field goal, 8:26. Drive: 12 plays, 57 yards in 7:22.

Team Stats

	EAGLES	GIANTS
1st Downs	18	15
3rd-Down Conversions	2-13	6-15
4th-Down Conversions	2-3	0-0
Punts-Average	6-42.0	6-35.7
Punts-Returns	1-8	3-53
Kickoffs-Returns	4-74	4-90
Interceptions-Returns	0-0	0-0
Penalties-Yards	7-41	3-15
Fumbles-Lost	1-1	2-2
Time of Possession	32:29	27:31
Total Net Yards	306	318
Total Plays	62	60
Net Yards Rushing	141	111
Rushes	28	27
Net Yards Passing	165	207
Comp.-Att.-Int.	20-31-0	17-31-0
Sacked-Yards Lost	3-14	2-12
Red Zone Efficiency	1/2-50%	0/3-0%

Giants receiver Plaxico Burress had seven receptions for 136 yards and a touchdown. *AP Images*

Fred Robbins celebrates his sack of Redskins quarterback Todd Collins. *Michael Appleton/Daily News*

GIANTS LOSE GAME, SHOCKEY TO REDSKINS

December 17, 2007 ◆ By Ralph Vacchiano, Daily News

THE FORMULA FOR the Giants seemed simple enough: Win and they'd be in the playoffs for the third straight season.

Now there's nothing simple about that at all.

Given a chance to rest easy over the final two games of the season, the Giants will instead live dangerously once again after they failed to throw a playoff-clinching party for their home fans Sunday night. They lost their third straight game at Giants Stadium, 22-10 to the Washington Redskins.

They also lost one of their most potent weapons, Jeremy Shockey, to a broken leg.

If the Giants (9-5) still plan on going to the playoffs, they'll either need some help or a win in Buffalo next Sunday. Otherwise, their fate will come down to their regular-season finale against the still-perfect New England Patriots.

Without Shockey, and considering they haven't topped 21 points in nearly two months, they don't seem capable of an upset like that.

"We could've made things easier on ourselves," said Michael Strahan. "We never seem to be able to do that."

> "WE COULD HAVE MADE THINGS EASIER ON OURSELVES. WE NEVER SEEM TO BE ABLE TO DO THAT."
> —MICHAEL STRAHAN

"Are we worried? No," added defensive end Justin Tuck. "But we don't feel good."

They felt downright miserable after falling into a 22-3 hole early in the third quarter against a Redskins team led by a 36-year-old quarterback making his first start in 10 seasons. Todd Collins wasn't very impressive, completing just 8 of 25 passes for 166 yards, but he was still better than Eli Manning, who completed 18 of 52 passes for 184 yards.

Manning's 34 incompletions were the most in the NFL in 40 years.

And Manning got an early start, misfiring on his first four passes and completing 6 of 21 for 51 yards in the first half. It wasn't all his fault as Manning was hurt by a cold, gusty wind that swirled around the half-empty stadium, and his butter-fingered teammates chipped in with nearly a dozen drops.

But he was bad enough to put his team in a 19-point hole before he started to warm up.

"In the first half we didn't have a lot going," a frustrated Tom Coughlin said. "We just did some things that didn't add up and didn't make a lot of

Giants running back Brandon Jacobs is knocked down by Washington defenders. Jacobs finished the game with 25 carries for 130 yards. *Michael Appleton/Daily News*

sense. I don't want to generalize and say they weren't smart, but we just didn't do what we had to do to win."

About the only thing the Giants had going for them was the running game, led by Brandon Jacobs' 130 yards. But he was nearly matched by Washington running back Clinton Portis (126 yards), and Jacobs hurt the Giants with four drops.

The defense didn't help either. After Collins started 0-for-8, the Giants let him complete back-to-back big passes — 36 yards to Santana Moss and 30 yards to tight end Todd Yoder, setting up 31-yard field goal that gave Washington a 6-0 lead.

Two drives later, Collins did it again, hitting Moss for a 34-yard gain down the sidelines. Three plays later, he pump-faked and handed the ball to Ladell Betts on a delayed draw up the middle, and then watched Betts run through four Giants defenders — linebacker Kawika Mitchell, safeties Craig Dahl and Michael Johnson, and cornerback Aaron Ross — en route to a 14-yard touchdown run and a 13-0 Washington lead.

The Redskins then took over the game by slicing through the Giants' defense on the opening

WEEK 15

	1st	2nd	3rd	4th	Final
REDSKINS	3	13	6	0	22
GIANTS	0	3	7	0	10

Scoring Summary

1st
REDSKINS Shaun Suisham, 49 yd field goal, 2:23. Drive: 6 plays, 20 yards in 2:24.

2nd
REDSKINS Shaun Suisham, 31 yd field goal, 10:12. Drive: 6 plays, 67 yards in 2:40.
REDSKINS Ladell Betts, 14 yd run (Shaun Suisham kick is good), 3:07. Drive: 6 plays, 50 yards in 2:05.
GIANTS Lawrence Tynes, 35 yd field goal, 1:16. Drive: 8 plays, 55 yards in 1:51.
REDSKINS Shaun Suisham, 28 yd field goal, 0:00. Drive: 7 plays, 62 yards in 1:16.

3rd
REDSKINS Clinton Portis, 5 yd run pass failed, 12:08. Drive: 5 plays, 46 yards in 2:52.
GIANTS Kevin Boss, 19 yd pass from Eli Manning (Lawrence Tynes kick is good), 4:37. Drive: 6 plays, 48 yards in 2:24.

Team Stats

	REDSKINS	GIANTS
1st Downs	14	20
3rd-Down Conversions	3-15	5-20
4th-Down Conversions	0-0	2-5
Punts-Average	9-37.6	7-34.1
Punts-Returns	4-1	3-20
Kickoffs-Returns	3-55	4-102
Interceptions-Returns	0-0	0-0
Penalties-Yards	4-35	3-35
Fumbles-Lost	0-0	1-1
Time of Possession	28:55	31:05
Total Net Yards	309	307
Total Plays	62	83
Net Yards Rushing	153	139
Rushes	35	28
Net Yards Passing	156	168
Comp.-Att.-Int.	8-25-0	18-52-0
Sacked-Yards Lost	2-10	2-16
Red Zone Efficiency	2/4-50%	1/2-50%

drive of the third quarter. They moved 46 yards in five plays in just 2:52, culminating in a five-yard touchdown by Portis that put them up 22-3.

Two plays later, injury was added to insult when the Giants lost Shockey. The injury occurred at the tail end of a Jacobs run when Amani Toomer rolled up the back of Shockey's left leg as the tight end was bent over awkwardly by Redskins linebacker H.B. Blades. Shockey had to be carried off the field and carted to the locker room, where he was diagnosed with a fractured left fibula.

He's expected to have surgery in the coming days.

"Anytime you lose a player of that quality at this time of the season is a huge loss," Coughlin said. "I feel very badly for him."

The Giants could end up feeling very badly for themselves, too. They did mount a brief rally when Manning fired a 19-yard touchdown pass to Shockey's replacement, rookie tight end Kevin Boss. The quarterback had the offense clicking on the Giants' next drive, too.

But when Lawrence Tynes missed a 38-yard field goal with 13:10 remaining, the Giants' best chance to make things at least interesting was lost.

Giants tight end Kevin Boss celebrates his fourth-quarter touchdown on a 19-yard pass from Eli Manning. *Michael Appleton/Daily News*

Instead, the whole season just got interesting.

"It's frustrating, no doubt," Coughlin said. "I think it would be frustrating anywhere. But to be at home, with what was at stake and what the consequences were?"

"Forget the playoffs," added right tackle Kareem McKenzie. "Right now it's about playing better football. We have to get this figured out and get it fixed."

Giants cornerback Corey Webster (23) celebrates his fourth-quarter touchdown on an interception with James Butler. *AP Images*

GIANTS STORM TO PLAYOFFS

December 24, 2007 ◆ By Ralph Vacchiano, Daily News

IN A GAME the Giants felt they absolutely had to win, they already were down two touchdowns before it was 10 minutes old. Then came the rains and the tropical storm-like winds.

In other words, the situation was perfect. The Giants do seem to play better with their backs against the wall.

"We're not going to ever quit," said receiver Amani Toomer. "We're always fighting to the end. So I don't think anybody was panicked."

Added linebacker Antonio Pierce: "This team hasn't folded all year."

The Giants didn't fold Sunday. They rallied from that early deficit and again from four points down in the fourth quarter to clinch an NFC wild-card berth with a 38-21 win over the Buffalo Bills.

The Giants will hit the road to play the Tampa Bay Buccaneers on either Jan. 5 or 6.

It was their seventh straight road win. And it gave them a 10-5 record, which might just be enough to lock up a contract extension for Tom Coughlin, their embattled coach who has now led them to the playoffs three straight years.

That hasn't happened since 1984-86 and it nearly didn't happen yesterday. Not only were the Giants down 14-0 with 5:31 left in the first quarter, but Eli Manning ended up doing his best Eli Manning impersonation by throwing two interceptions and fumbling five times (losing two).

But unlike last week, when Manning threw 53 times on a windy night in losing to the Redskins, the Giants rediscovered their running attack. In 30-mph winds, a steady rain and late snow, Brandon Jacobs rushed for a career-high 145 yards and two touchdowns before leaving with a sprained ankle, and rookie Ahmad Bradshaw had 151 yards on 17 carries, including an 88-yard touchdown run in the fourth quarter. The Giants rushed 47 times for 291 yards, their highest total in 48 years.

Amani Toomer caught five of Manning's seven completions for 99 yards, including three on third downs. Linebacker Kawika Mitchell — the only starter GM Jerry Reese brought in as a free agent — returned an interception 20 yards for a touchdown in the fourth quarter to give the Giants the lead for good at 24-21. Corey Webster, who lost his job earlier this season and has been buried on the bench ever since, sealed it with 5:50 remaining with a 34-yard interception return for a score.

"That's what I've been trying to say from Day One," Pierce said. "This is a team. This ain't a one-man show."

The Giants needed a full-team effort after the way the game started, with two touchdown passes by Bills quarterback Trent Edwards (9-for-26, 161 yards) on the first two drives. The Giants might have been buried by that early if they didn't get two big breaks — a fumbled snap on a punt that led to a 6-yard touchdown run by Jacobs, and a roughing-the-punter penalty on the Bills (7-8) that set up Jacobs' 43-yard touchdown run.

Add in a 42-yard field goal by Lawrence Tynes, and the Giants led 17-14 at the half. But these Giants just aren't comfortable playing with a lead. They gave it back when Manning's first pass of the second half was tipped into the hands of Bills linebacker Keith Ellison. That set up a 3-yard touchdown run by Marshawn Lynch.

And things would get worse. On the next possession, the Giants drove to the Buffalo 1, but came up empty on four straight runs. On the next drive, they reached the Buffalo 11, only to see Manning (7-for-15, 111 yards) — on the first play of the fourth quarter — get picked off again.

As the defense ran out onto the field, Mitchell told his teammates he was going to score a touchdown. Two plays later, an Edwards pass bounced off Lee Evans' shoulder, and Mitchell was able to back up his words.

"We needed a boost," Coughlin said. "And he gave it to us."

They got another one from their running game, which was dominant in the second half, accounting for 31 of the Giants' 34 plays and 208 yards — a dramatic change from their ill-conceived, 53-pass attack against Washington last weekend. The biggest run came with 6:12 left, right after Bradshaw — the seventh-round pick out of Marshall who had all of six NFL carries coming into the game — told his quarterback, "I'm going to take it to the house and end this game."

"Sure enough, he was able to do it," Manning said. "That's the kind of attitude that you want from your running back. He's a playmaker."

Webster added the punctuation mark 22 seconds later, but by then the playoff celebration already was on. A few minutes later, Coughlin got the coldest Gatorade shower of his life. "It was the chunks of ice that gave me some mixed thoughts about exactly what the intentions were," the relieved coach said with a smile.

Now the Giants don't have to worry about getting help to reach the playoffs, or needing to beat the undefeated New England Patriots on Saturday night.

"It was a game we knew we had to win," Coughlin said. "It says something about a team when they know they have a chance to secure a playoff spot and we play through some adversity."

Said Toomer: "Say what you want about us, but we're always in the playoffs."

WEEK 16

	1st	2nd	3rd	4th	Final
BILLS	14	0	7	0	21
GIANTS	0	17	0	21	38

Scoring Summary

1st

BILLS — Michael Gaines, 3 yd pass from Trent Edwards (Rian Lindell kick is good), 10:24. Drive: 7 plays, 60 yards in 4:36.

BILLS — Lee Evans, 4 yd pass from Trent Edwards (Rian Lindell kick is good), 5:31. Drive: 6 plays, 66 yards in 3:01.

2nd

GIANTS — Brandon Jacobs, 6 yd run (Lawrence Tynes kick is good), 11:38. Drive: 5 plays, 23 yards in 1:58.

GIANTS — Brandon Jacobs, 43 yd run (Lawrence Tynes kick is good), 8:32. Drive: 4 plays, 57 yards in 1:47.

GIANTS — Lawrence Tynes, 42 yd field goal, 2:35. Drive: 7 plays, 32 yards in 4:16.

3rd

BILLS — Marshawn Lynch, 3 yd run (Rian Lindell kick is good), 13:54. Drive: 2 plays, 31 yards in 0:51.

4TH

GIANTS — Kawika Mitchell, 20 yd interception return (Lawrence Tynes kick is good), 14:05.

GIANTS — Ahmad Bradshaw, 88 yd run (Lawrence Tynes kick is good), 6:12. Drive: 1 play, 88 yards in 0:15.

GIANTS — Corey Webster, 34 yd interception return (Lawrence Tynes kick is good), 5:50.

Team Stats

	BILLS	GIANTS
1st Downs	16	17
3rd-Down Conversions	1-9	6-14
4th-Down Conversions	0-1	0-2
Punts-Average	7-38.1	3-40.0
Punts-Returns	1-20	5-13
Kickoffs-Returns	3-65	4-99
Interceptions-Returns	2-5	3-81
Penalties-Yards	6-45	4-25
Fumbles-Lost	4-1	5-2
Time of Possession	25:55	34:05
Total Net Yards	244	383
Total Plays	57	64
Net Yards Rushing	117	289
Rushes	28	47
Net Yards Passing	127	94
Comp.-Att.-Int.	9-26-3	7-15-2
Sacked-Yards Lost	3-34	2-17
Red Zone Efficiency	3/3-100%	1/4-25%

Kawika Mitchell's interception turned into a touchdown early in the fourth quarter to give the Giants a slim lead. *AP Images*

Patriots wide receiver Randy Moss gestures to fans during New England's 38-35 victory against New York.
AP Images

A PERFECT PREPARATION FOR PLAYOFFS

December 30, 2007 ◆ By Ralph Vacchiano, Daily News

NO ONE DUMPED a bucket of Gatorade on Tom Coughlin on Saturday night, and there was no champagne in the locker room to celebrate the Giants' moral victory.

But they still were pretty pleased with themselves after their 38-35 loss to the New England Patriots at Giants Stadium. While they couldn't stop the Pats' pursuit of perfection, at least the Giants proved they're pretty good, too.

"Everybody can stop talking about how this is a bad 10-6 team now," linebacker Antonio Pierce said. "Maybe now somebody will consider us a Super Bowl contender."

Maybe they will, after the Giants came as close as anyone has all season to knocking off the 16-0 Patriots. The Giants had a 12-point lead in the third quarter — the largest anyone has had on New England all season. And the 35 points the Giants scored were the most against the Patriots this year.

Sure, they couldn't hang on to a 28-23 fourth-quarter lead. And yes, the Patriots scored 22 straight points before the Giants tacked on a touchdown with 1:04 remaining. But Eli Manning was spectacular. The Giants' defense held its ground.

> "EVERYBODY CAN STOP TALKING ABOUT HOW THIS IS A BAD 10-6 TEAM NOW."
> —ANTONIO PIERCE

And Coughlin loved the way his team fought right up until the end — a perfect way for it to prepare for a first-round playoff game next weekend in Tampa.

"There's nothing but positives," Coughlin said. "I told the players that in playing this game, everything would be positive. There would be no negatives. That's pretty much the way I feel.

"I don't know of any better way of getting prepared to play the playoffs."

That's why Coughlin decided to play his starters in what was a meaningless game for the Giants, and play them right up until the end. He kept his foot on the gas, even after losing three starters to injury — linebacker Kawika Mitchell and center Shaun O'Hara in the first half, and cornerback Sam Madison in the second.

He was rewarded by the Giants' finest offensive performance of the season. Manning completed 22 of 32 passes for 251 yards and four touchdowns, his most since opening night in a loss to the Cowboys. The Giants got a 74-yard kickoff return for a touchdown by Domenik Hixon on just his third return of the season for Big Blue.

And Coughlin got a terrific effort from a defense

Giants running back Brandon Jacobs (27) celebrates after scoring on a 7-yard pass from Eli Manning.
Ron Antonelli/Daily News

that held off the Patriots' record-setting offense deep into the third quarter. Before the Patriots exploded for 22 points in the final 19 minutes, the Patriots' attack had consisted of three field goals and one touchdown pass from Tom Brady to Randy Moss.

"Nobody wants to hear, 'We played hard, but we didn't win the game,'" Coughlin said. "But what they do need to hear is they made a great effort, they prepared, they sacrificed, they were excited about playing this team. Their heart was definitely in the right place."

"It strengthened our belief in our football team," added defensive end Justin Tuck. "It reinstilled in us that we have a pretty good team ourselves."

The Giants felt so good about themselves that Manning said, "I've never seen a locker room so upbeat after a loss." And there were very few players who, like Amani Toomer, said, "I don't believe in the whole valiant effort thing."

For the most part, the Giants were basking in the glow of their near-victory, and reveling in the momentum they now will carry to Tampa Bay.

"I feel like everything came together for us," said running back Brandon Jacobs. "This is the team, right here, that's going to be out here for the rest of the year."

"If we can go out and play like that, with that intensity each week," added Plaxico Burress, "we can win a lot of football games."

Patriots quarterback Tom Brady is brought down by Giants defenders.
Ron Antonelli/Daily News

Brandon Jacobs dives into the end zone in the first quarter. *Ron Antonelli/Daily News*

WEEK 17

	1st	2nd	3rd	4th	Final
PATRIOTS	3	13	7	15	38
GIANTS	7	14	7	7	35

Scoring Summary

1st

GIANTS — Brandon Jacobs, 7 yd pass from Eli Manning (Lawrence Tynes kick is good), 10:59. Drive: 7 plays, 74 yards in 4:01.

PATS — Stephen Gostkowski, 37 yd field goal, 5:19. Drive: 12 plays, 54 yards in 5:40.

2nd

PATS — Randy Moss, 4 yd pass from Tom Brady (Stephen Gostkowski kick is good), 14:55. Drive: 8 plays, 50 yards in 3:41.

GIANTS — Domenik Hixon, 74 yd kick return (Lawrence Tynes kick is good), 14:44.

PATS — Stephen Gostkowski, 45 yd field goal, 9:59. Drive: 8 plays, 39 yards in 4:45.

PATS — Stephen Gostkowski, 37 yd field goal, 1:59. Drive: 11 plays, 61 yards in 5:41.

GIANTS — Kevin Boss, 3 yd pass from Eli Manning (Lawrence Tynes kick is good), 0:13. Drive: 8 plays, 85 yards in 1:46.

3rd

GIANTS — Plaxico Burress, 19 yd pass from Eli Manning (Lawrence Tynes kick is good), 9:12. Drive: 7 plays, 60 yards in 4:10.

PATS — Laurence Maroney, 6 yd run (Stephen Gostkowski kick is good), 4:00. Drive: 8 plays, 73 yards in 5:12.

4th

PATS — Randy Moss, 65 yd pass from Tom Brady (Laurence Maroney run), 11:06. Drive: 3 plays, 65 yards in 0:23.

PATS — Laurence Maroney, 5 yd run (Stephen Gostkowski kick is good), 4:36. Drive: 9 plays, 52 yards in 5:17.

GIANTS — Plaxico Burress, 3 yd pass from Eli Manning (Lawrence Tynes kick is good), 1:04. Drive: 11 plays, 68 yards in 3:32.

Team Stats

	GIANTS	PATS
1st Downs	19	27
3rd-Down Conversions	6-10	6-13
4th-Down Conversions	0-0	1-1
Punts-Average	4-37.5	2-40.5
Punts-Returns	2-2	2-10
Kickoffs-Returns	8-221	4-88
Interceptions-Returns	0-0	1-0
Penalties-Yards	5-53	5-42
Fumbles-Lost	1-0	0-0
Time of Possession	23:42	36:18
Total Net Yards	316	390
Total Plays	52	69
Net Yards Rushing	79	44
Rushes	19	26
Net Yards Passing	237	346
Comp.-Att.-Int.	22-32-1	32-42-0
Sacked-Yards Lost	1-14	1-10
Red Zone Efficiency	4/4-100%	3/5-60%

PLAYOFFS

Giants running back Brandon Jacobs scrambles into the end zone for his first of two touchdowns in the second quarter. *Corey Sipkin/Daily News*

GIANTS BEAT BUCS TO SET UP COWBOYS REMATCH

January 7, 2008 ◆ By Ralph Vacchiano, Daily News

THE GIANTS' PREVIOUS playoff victory still "seemed like yesterday" to Michael Strahan, until somebody told him it hadn't happened in seven long years.

"If I had ever thought about the total time frame," Strahan said, "I would've quit a long time ago."

Now, of course, there's no reason for Strahan to hang 'em up, because there's no quit in these Giants. They beat the Tampa Bay Buccaneers, 24-14, Sunday in the NFC wild-card playoffs for their first playoff victory since the 2000 season. They head to Dallas on Sunday for another rematch with the NFC East-champion Cowboys.

And they will do it in what for all but two players in their locker room is uncharted territory:

The second round.

"We're coming to work next week," said guard Chris Snee. "That's something we haven't been able to do the last couple of years."

The only current Giants who were on the team the last time the Giants were still working this late were Strahan and receiver Amani Toomer. They had been bounced out of the first round three straight times and in each of the last two years — twice at the hands of Jeff Garcia, who was the Bucs quarterback Sunday.

But none of that mattered as the Giants (11-6) won their eighth straight game on the road by pounding Garcia with their league-best pass rush, hitting him 11 times and sacking him once, disrupting what little offense the Bucs (9-8) had. That opened the door for Eli Manning to win the first playoff game of his career with a workmanlike, mistake-free performance (20-for-27, 185 yards, two touchdowns, no interceptions) on a warm, sunny day against the No. 1 pass defense in the league.

"My thought process was to play really safe, don't force anything," Manning said. "They do a great job getting turnovers. You want to get the ball out quick. Don't throw interceptions and don't get back there too long where they can cause a fumble."

Actually, it was the Bucs who committed all the turnovers — three in all, and all in the second half of a game they trailed only 14-7 at halftime. That included two interceptions for Garcia, who had been picked off just four times all year. The Bucs even opened the second half with a fumble on the kickoff that was recovered by Giants cornerback Corey Webster. That led to a 25-yard field goal by Lawrence Tynes that gave the Giants a 17-7 lead.

The turning point came on the ensuing Bucs drive. Garcia (23-for-39, 207 yards) moved the Bucs to the Giants' 27-yard line, where they went for it all and sent Joey Galloway streaking toward the end zone. But the pass was slightly underthrown, which enabled Webster — a former starter who only played because Sam Madison (abdominal strain) was hurt — to leap and pick it off.

The Giants didn't score off that turnover, but they did put the game out of reach on their next drive — a 15-play, 92-yard march to a 4-yard touchdown pass from Manning to Toomer (seven catches, 74 yards) that consumed more than 8-$\frac{1}{2}$ minutes. The drive started late in the third quarter, and when it was over the Giants were ahead 24-7 and there was only 8:03 to play.

"Give credit to this offense to be able to do something like that against the No. 1 defense in the league," Snee said.

It was amazing they were able to do that given the tough time they had against the Bucs' defense, especially early. The Giants were in a 7-0 hole and didn't pick up a first down until early in the second quarter. Brandon Jacobs may have scored two touchdowns, but he had so much trouble (13 carries, 34 yards) that he had to be relieved by rookie running back Ahmad Bradshaw (17-66) later in the game.

"Early on we just knew that it wasn't going to be easy," said left tackle David Diehl. "But we knew if we kept sticking to it, sooner or later it was going to break."

It eventually did, and the Giants were able to build a big enough lead that a late touchdown pass from Garcia didn't matter. The Giants sealed it with 1:53 remaining on a leaping interception from R.W. McQuarters, who barely managed to get two feet down inside the sidelines.

"It was a struggle at first," said Tom Coughlin, who undoubtedly guaranteed himself a contract extension with his first playoff win as Giants coach, and his first since the 1999 season with Jacksonville. "It wasn't easy, no doubt about it. But we have good character as a team. We have good leadership. We have physical and mental toughness. We have a resiliency."

Now they have a playoff victory to go with all that, too.

"I don't know if it's relief, but I am excited," said defensive end Justin Tuck. "If you say 'relief' you're saying we came down here not expecting to win."

"It's been a progressive thing," added Coughlin. "But it finally got done today."

Giants defensive end Osi Umenyiora shares a smile with head coach Tom Coughlin during the second half. *Corey Sipkin/Daily News*

Giants running back Ahmad Bradshaw gained a team-best 66 yards on 17 carries against Tampa Bay.
Corey Sipkin/Daily News

NFC WILDCARD

	1st	2nd	3rd	4th	Final
BUCCANEERS	7	0	0	7	14
GIANTS	0	14	3	7	24

Scoring Summary

1st
BUCS   Earnest Graham, 1 yd run (Matt Bryant kick is good), 1:49. Drive: 10 plays, 54 yards in 5:13.

2nd
GIANTS   Brandon Jacobs, 5 yd pass from Eli Manning (Lawrence Tynes kick is good), 10:02. Drive: 8 plays, 53 yards in 4:04.
GIANTS   Brandon Jacobs, 8 yd run (Lawrence Tynes kick is good), 4:06. Drive: 7 plays, 65 yards in 4:23.

3rd
GIANTS   Lawrence Tynes, 25 yd field goal, 9:56. Drive: 9 plays, 23 yards in 4:54.

4TH
GIANTS   Amani Toomer, 4 yd pass from Eli Manning (Lawrence Tynes kick is good), 8:03. Drive: 15 plays, 92 yards in 8:37.
BUCS   Alex Smith, 6 yd pass from Jeff Garcia (Matt Bryant kick is good), 3:25. Drive: 12 plays, 88 yards in 4:38.

Team Stats

	BUCCANEERS	GIANTS
1st Downs	20	16
3rd-Down Conversions	9-14	5-12
4th-Down Conversions	0-0	0-0
Punts-Average	5-36.8	6-44.5
Punts-Returns	2-5	2-15
Kickoffs-Returns	5-106	3-54
Interceptions-Returns	0-0	2-0
Penalties-Yards	4-25	5-41
Fumbles-Lost	2-1	0-0
Time of Possession	26:29	33:31
Total Net Yards	271	277
Total Plays	62	58
Net Yards Rushing	69	100
Rushes	22	30
Net Yards Passing	202	177
Comp.-Att.-Int.	23-39-2	20-27-0
Sacked-Yards Lost	1-5	1-8
Red Zone Efficiency	2/2-100%	3/4-75%

Michael Strahan, who led Giants defenders with seven solo tackles, celebrates as New York knocks off Dallas to advance to the NFC Championship. *Linda Cataffo/Daily News*

THIRD TIMES A CHARM AGAINST COWBOYS

January 14, 2008 ◆ By Ralph Vacchiano, Daily News

AFTER LISTENING ALL week long to the trash talk coming out of Dallas, the Giants finally got their chance to hit the Cowboys in their big, fat mouths.

The Giants sent Tony Romo back to the beach with Jessica Simpson, ruined Terrell Owens' popcorn and stuffed Patrick Crayton's foot in his sizeable mouth when they stunned Dallas, 21-17, in the NFC divisional playoffs Sunday at Texas Stadium.

It was the Giants' NFL-record ninth straight road win and their first win in three tries against the Cowboys this season.

"That's what happens with people like that," said Giants linebacker Kawika Mitchell. "They stick their foot in their mouth and they end up going home early. We're still in the dance and we'll be having some fun, while they'll be watching us on TV."

Thanks to a quietly efficient performance by Eli Manning and a huge second half from the Giants' defense, it will be the Giants (12-6) who will be playing the Green Bay Packers in the NFC Championship Game at Lambeau Field on Sunday night. It will be the Giants' first appearance in the title game since their 2000 Super Bowl run.

Manning got them there by playing another mistake-free game, completing 12 of 18 passes for 163 yards and two touchdowns, both to veteran Amani Toomer (four catches, 80 yards). He also led the Giants on a short drive early in the fourth quarter that resulted in Brandon Jacobs' go-ahead 1-yard touchdown run.

But it was the Giants' exhausted and depleted defense that deserves credit for this win after shutting down Owens (four catches, 49 yards), keeping Romo in check (18-for-36, 201 yards) and holding the Cowboys to just three points and 141 yards in the second half.

They were at their best in the final minutes, when rookie Geoff Pope was forced into action because Aaron Ross was out (shoulder) and first-year pro Dave Tollefson was on the field because Michael Strahan had strained his groin. Still, the Giants survived a Cowboys drive that started on the Dallas 44, thanks to a huge sack by Mitchell

> "WE'RE STILL IN THE DANCE AND WE'LL BE HAVING SOME FUN, WHILE THEY'LL BE WATCHING US ON TV."
> —KAWIKA MITCHELL

Giants linebacker Antonio Pierce applies pressure to scrambling Cowboys quarterback Tony Romo.
Corey Sipkin/Daily News

"IT WAS A GREAT JOB
BY OUR DEFENSE. IT'S NOT
EASY TO STOP THOSE GUYS."
—ELI MANNING

and two huge penalties by the Cowboys (illegal formation and intentional grounding).

The last drive came down to what linebacker Antonio Pierce called "the longest 31 seconds of my life." The final stand came when cornerback R.W. McQuarters, who had ended the Giants' playoff-opening win in Tampa with an interception, stepped in front of Terry Glenn in the end zone and picked off Romo's pass with just nine seconds to play.

"You're a little nervous (at the end) because when you look at Dallas, they always seem to find a way to win close games," Manning said. "It was a great job by our defense. It's not easy to stop those guys."

It wasn't easy at all in the first half, when Marion Barber (27 carries, 129 yards) powered a

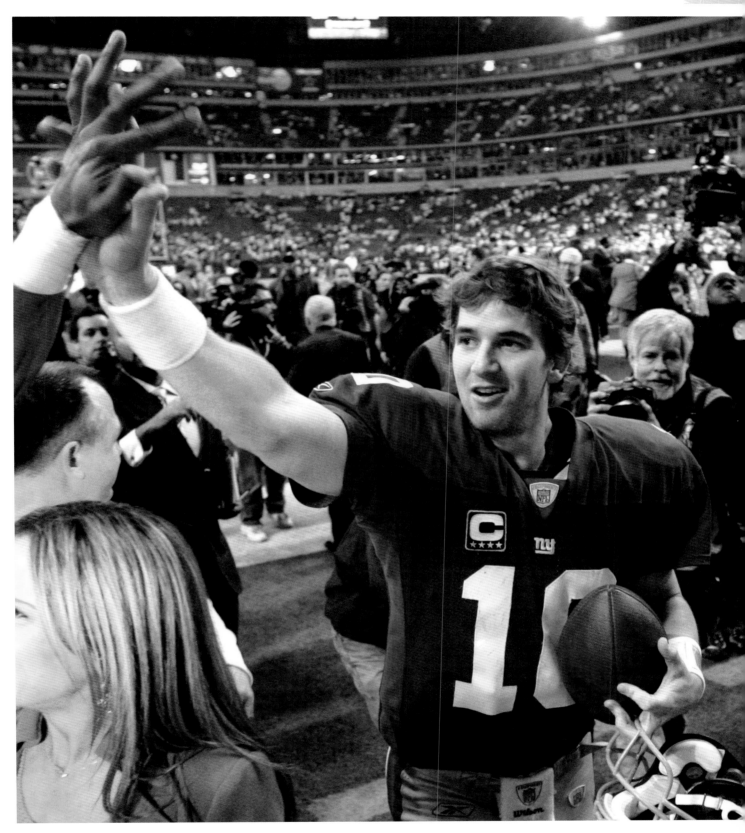

Eli Manning high-fives a teammate as he leaves the field following the Giants' 21-17 victory against the Cowboys. *Corey Sipkin/Daily News*

Giants wide receiver Amani Toomer hauls in a 4-yard touchdown reception in the second quarter. Toomer finished the game with 80 receiving yards and two TDs. *Corey Sipkin/Daily News*

Cowboys offense that oddly decided to stick mostly on the ground, despite the depleted nature of the Giants' secondary (starting corner Sam Madison and nickel back Kevin Dockery were both inactive). Barber had 101 of his yards in the first half, and the Cowboys took a 14-7 lead with two impressive drives.

The second drive, in fact, ate up most of the second quarter. The Cowboys took 20 plays and ate 10:28 off the clock. When Barber plunged over the goal line for a 1-yard touchdown, the Giants' defense was exhausted and there were just 53 seconds left.

Then came what Pierce called the turning point because he could see on the sidelines, "We really had our heads down."

"They had all the momentum and our defense was gassed," Manning added. "Not a whole lot was going our way."

Then, everything changed. Manning led the Giants on one of the finest drives of his career. He quickly marched them 71 yards on seven plays in just 46 seconds, getting two huge catches from rookie Steve Smith and another from rookie tight end Kevin Boss.

The finale came on a bullet pass over the middle to Toomer, who reached around safety Ken Hamlin and lunged for the end zone, a 4-yard touchdown that tied the game at 14-14 with just seven seconds.

Toomer, who had opened the game with a 52-yard touchdown reception on the Giants' first drive, was so confident at that point that on the way to the locker room he caught up to Strahan, who might retire after the season, and told him, "This will not be the last game I play with you."

It won't be because, after the Cowboys took a 17-14 third-quarter lead on a Nick Fold field goal, the Giants' defense didn't break again. And eventually the Giants got a huge, 25-yard punt return from McQuarters to set them up at the Dallas 37 late in the quarter.

Five plays later, Jacobs gave the Giants their first lead since early in the second quarter.

About 13 minutes after that, the Giants were on their way to a happy locker room, where they had hung a banner that read "Getcha popcorn ready!" — Owens' favorite phrase.

The Giants then reveled in the fact that they have another game to prepare for, and that they don't have to listen to trash talk coming out of Dallas anymore, especially Crayton's contention that the visitors were the ones guilty of talking trash.

"We do have the salt for everyone who was a little salty towards us," Pierce said. "We have enough butter and salt for all of that popcorn."

"Not that we needed any motivation," said defensive end Justin Tuck. "But you just don't say things like that to a hungry football team."

NFC DIVISIONAL

	1st	2nd	3rd	4th	Final
COWBOYS	0	14	3	0	17
GIANTS	7	7	0	7	21

Scoring Summary

1st
GIANTS Amani Toomer, 52 yd pass from Eli Manning (Lawrence Tynes kick is good). Drive: 6 plays, 77 yards in 3:10. 11:50.

2nd
COWBOYS Terrell Owens, 5 yd pass from Tony Romo (Nick Folk kick is good), 14:56. Drive: 9 plays, 96 yards in 4:57.
COWBOYS Marion Barber, 1 yd run (Nick Folk kick is good), 0:53. Drive: 20 plays, 90 yards in 10:28.
GIANTS Amani Toomer, 4 yd pass from Eli Manning (Lawrence Tynes kick is good), 0:07. Drive: 7 plays, 71 yards in 0:46.

3rd
COWBOYS Nick Folk, 34 yd field goal, 6:53. Drive: 14 plays, 62 yards in 8:07.

4TH
GIANTS Brandon Jacobs, 1 yd run (Lawrence Tynes kick is good), 13:29. Drive: 6 plays, 37 yards in 2:24.

Team Stats

	COWBOYS	GIANTS
1st Downs	23	16
3rd-Down Conversions	10-16	4-9
4th-Down Conversions	0-1	0-0
Punts-Average	4-47.3	5-42.8
Punts-Returns	2-8	1-25
Kickoffs-Returns	4-88	4-106
Interceptions-Returns	0-0	1-0
Penalties-Yards	11-84	3-25
Fumbles-Lost	1-0	0-0
Time of Possession	36:30	23:30
Total Net Yards	336	230
Total Plays	71	44
Net Yards Rushing	154	90
Rushes	33	23
Net Yards Passing	182	140
Comp.-Att.-Int.	18-36-1	12-18-0
Sacked-Yards Lost	2-19	3-23
Red Zone Efficiency	2/3-66%	2/2-100%

Giants place kicker Lawrence Tynes kicks the game-winning, 47-yard field goal in overtime at Lambeau Field. *Corey Sipkin/Daily News*

GIANTS SHOCK PACKERS IN OVERTIME

January 21, 2008 ◆ By Ralph Vacchiano, Daily News

IN THE SPLIT second it took Tom Coughlin to decide to go for the field goal that would send the Giants to the Super Bowl, he turned to find the decision already had been made. Lawrence Tynes, who had earlier missed two potential game-winners, never waited to hear Coughlin tell him to get out there.

He already was out on the field.

"I knew I could get it there," said the ice-veined kicker. "He was going to have to pull me off that field."

Coughlin never did, and Tynes delivered as promised with a 47-yard field goal that rocked the NFL. It came 2:35 into overtime of the NFC Championship Game last night, through an icy, Wisconsin wind at historic and frigid Lambeau Field. And when the ball cleared the crossbar, the Giants had improbably knocked off the Green Bay Packers, 23-20.

Now their wild ride will continue on Feb. 3 in Glendale, Ariz., when they get a second shot at the undefeated New England Patriots, this time in Super Bowl XLII.

And the triumph that sent them west was as incredible as their season itself, coming on one of the coldest days in the 83-year history of their franchise. Despite a kickoff temperature of minus-1 and a wind-chill of 23-below, they got a terrific game from resurgent quarterback Eli Manning (21-of-40, 254 yards), a brilliant day from Plaxico Burress (11 catches, 154 yards), and a clutch performance by a defense that picked off Brett Favre twice, the second time — by Corey Webster — on the second play of overtime.

But it was Tynes who embodied the resiliency of a Giants team that has won 10 straight on the road, and became the first NFC team to ever reach the Super Bowl by winning three straight playoff

Giants fans root on New York against Green Bay.
Robert Sabo/Daily News

games away from home. He missed a potential game-winning, 43-yarder with 6:37 remaining. Then he missed a 36-yarder, thanks in part to a bad snap, as the clock expired in the fourth.

But he was bailed out by Webster, who stepped in front of Donald Driver and picked off Favre (19-for-35, 236 yards) 56 seconds into overtime. Four plays later, on a fourth-and-5 from the Green Bay 29, Tynes came through.

"Before he went to kick the last one, Jerry (Reese, the Giants' GM) turned to me and said, 'He's making it,'" said Giants co-owner John Mara. "I thought, 'I don't know ... 47 yards in a minus-25 wind chill?'"

"I kidded with Lawrence that we just needed to move the ball back for him," said a red-faced Coughlin, who will coach in his first Super Bowl after three appearances in a conference championship game. "It was a little too close before."

Typical Giants: They do everything the hard

"I KIDDED WITH LAWRENCE (TYNES) THAT WE JUST NEEDED TO MOVE THE BALL BACK FOR HIM." —TOM COUGHLIN

way. They could have made this game much easier on themselves the way they moved the ball (380 total yards). But early on they settled for field goals instead of touchdowns. And with the help of a 90-yard TD pass from Favre to Driver in the second quarter, the Packers went into halftime with a 10-6 lead.

From there, it was back and forth. A 1-yard run by Brandon Jacobs (21 carries, 67 yards) in the third was answered by a 12-yard touchdown pass from Favre to Donald Lee — a score that was set up by a boneheaded personal foul on cornerback Sam Madison after the Giants appeared to have stopped the Pack in its tracks.

Then, after the Giants took a 20-17 lead on a 4-yard run by rookie Ahmad Bradshaw (16 carries,

Giants running back Ahmad Bradshaw breaks through the Packers defense for a 48-yard run into the end zone during the fourth quarter. The TD was nullified by an offensive holding penalty.
Michael Appleton/Daily News

Giants cornerback Corey Webster returns his overtime interception nine yards to set up the Giants' winning drive. *Corey Sipkin/Daily News*

63 yards) with 2:12 remaining in the third, they nearly iced the game in the fourth when R.W. McQuarters, deep inside Giants territory, picked off an errant Favre pass.

But on his return, McQuarters was stripped by ex-Giants running back Ryan Grant and Packers tackle Mark Tauscher recovered at the 19. Three plays later, Crosby hit a 37-yard field goal to tie the game at 20-20 with 11:46 to play.

That set the stage for Tynes, who came dangerously close to joining Trey Junkin at the top of the Giants' all-time list of playoff chokers. Instead, given a third chance to redeem himself by booting a frozen football ("It was like kicking cardboard," he said), Tynes nailed the game-winner, sprinted down the field and ran right up the tunnel.

"I just wanted to get out of the cold," Tynes said.

"It seems like we like to put ourselves in these situations," said Manning, who is on his way to his first Super Bowl one year after his brother, Peyton, reached (and won) his. "We can't make the short ones, we can't win at home. But we can win on the road and make the 47-yarders in overtime."

"It's Giants football," added receiver Amani Toomer. "We want to make sure our fans have some good, healthy blood pressure going into our games."

The blood will be pumping for the next two weeks, as the Giants prepare to take on a Patriots team that beat them, 38-35, at Giants Stadium back on Dec. 29. It was a confidence-building performance for the Giants, who played the Pats as well as anyone.

And they are undoubtedly relishing their chance to face them again.

But that's for later. Last night, with the George Halas Trophy being passed around, the Giants preferred to bask in the glow of their first NFC championship in seven seasons.

"We're here," Manning said. "And I think we're deserving of it."

"The real key has been the heart of this team," Coughlin added. "Their heart is in the right place."

NFC CHAMPIONSHIP

	1st	2nd	3rd	4th	OT	Final
PACKERS	0	10	7	3	0	20
GIANTS	3	3	14	0	3	23

Scoring Summary

1st
GIANTS Lawrence Tynes, 29 yd field goal, 4:50. Drive: 14 plays, 71 yards in 7:48.

2nd
GIANTS Lawrence Tynes, 37 yd field goal, 11:41. Drive: 7 plays, 38 yards in 3:04.
PACKERS Donald Driver, 90 yd pass from Brett Favre (Mason Crosby kick is good), 11:18. Drive: 1 plays, 90 yards in 0:23.
PACKERS Mason Crosby, 36 yd field goal, 1:30. Drive: 8 plays, 29 yards in 2:58.

3rd
GIANTS Brandon Jacobs, 1 yd run (Lawrence Tynes kick is good), 7:56. Drive: 12 plays, 69 yards in 7:04.
PACKERS Donald Lee, 12 yd pass from Brett Favre (Mason Crosby kick is good), 5:00. Drive: 6 plays, 39 yards in 2:56.
GIANTS Ahmad Bradshaw, 4 yd run (Lawrence Tynes kick is good), 2:12. Drive: 7 plays, 57 yards in 2:48.

4TH
PACKERS Mason Crosby, 37 yd field goal, 11:46.

OT
GIANTS Lawrence Tynes, 47 yd field goal, 12:25. Drive: 4 plays, 5 yards in 1:39.

Team Stats

	PACKERS	GIANTS
1st Downs	13	24
3rd-Down Conversions	1-10	6-16
4th-Down Conversions	0-0	0-1
Punts-Average	6-32.2	4-32.5
Punts-Returns	2-1	4-24
Kickoffs-Returns	5-103	5-121
Interceptions-Returns	0-0	2-20
Penalties-Yards	7-37	6-50
Fumbles-Lost	1-0	5-1
Time of Possession	22:34	40:01
Total Net Yards	264	377
Total Plays	49	81
Net Yards Rushing	28	134
Rushes	14	39
Net Yards Passing	236	243
Comp.-Att.-Int.	19-35-2	21-40-0
Sacked-Yards Lost	0-0	2-8
Red Zone Efficiency	1/3-33%	2/5-40%

SUPER BOWL

Giants receiver David Tyree falls to the ground, the football pinned to his helmet, to complete a spectacular 32-yard catch during the Giants' game-winning drive late in the fourth quarter. *Ron Antonelli/Daily News*

GIANTS STUN PATRIOTS TO WIN SUPER BOWL

February 5, 2008 ◆ By Ralph Vacchiano, Daily News

THE IMPERFECT GIANTS pulled off the perfect upset on Sunday night.

In what will go down as one of the biggest shockers in the history of the NFL, the surprising Giants ended their wildest season ever by stopping the New England Patriots' quest for perfection. They stunned the previously undefeated Pats, 17-14, in Super Bowl XLII to win their third Super Bowl championship and first in 17 years.

And they did it in typical heart-stopping fashion, as Eli Manning, the Super Bowl MVP, twice led them back from fourth-quarter deficits. Even after he threw the game-winning touchdown pass to Plaxico Burress with 35 seconds remaining, the Giants' defense had to withstand one last assault by the Patriots' record-setting offense.

When they did, the Patriots (18-1) had fallen from the ranks of the unbeaten, setting off a celebration that will stretch from Miami, home of the '72 Dolphins — still the lone unbeaten team in NFL history — right up the Canyon of Heroes tomorrow.

"We were trying not to make this another feel-good story or another Patriots dynasty story," defensive end Michael Strahan said. "We were try-ing to start our own dynasty. A New York Giants dynasty."

"We shocked the world," added linebacker Antonio Pierce. "But not ourselves."

In what co-owner John Mara called "the greatest victory in the history of this franchise, without question," the Giants (14-6) won their 11th straight game away from Giants Stadium. In doing so, they backed up a week of tough talk and guarantees with a dominating defense that spent much of the night pounding Tom Brady into the turf. They hit him nine times and recorded five sacks, including two by defensive end Justin Tuck.

That pressure on Brady created just enough room for Manning to punctuate his breakout season with his sixth fourth-quarter comeback of the year and the 10th of his career.

> "WE SHOCKED THE WORLD.
> BUT NOT OURSELVES."
> —ANTONIO PIERCE

The final drive was remarkable, including a play that might just be the Super Bowl highlight of all time as well the signature of Manning's early career. On third-and-5 from the Giants' 44 with just 1:15 remaining, he fought his way out of what looked like a sure sack, hands stretching his jersey along the way, and fired a rainbow pass down the field to David Tyree.

Tyree out-jumped Patriots safety Rodney Harrison, pinned the ball against his helmet, and held on for a 32-yard catch he called "supernatural."

Four plays later, Manning found Burress slipping behind cornerback Ellis Hobbs in the end zone for a 13-yard touchdown pass that put away the Super Bowl.

"Some things just don't make sense," Tyree said. "I guess you could put that catch up there with those."

The whole fourth quarter didn't make sense to anyone but the Giants. They entered the quarter trailing 7-3 on a night when their defense was holding the best offense in NFL history in check. Manning and the offense, though, couldn't get anything going — at least not to that point.

But Manning — who was 19-of-34 for 255 yards and joined brother Peyton as the first back-to-back Super Bowl MVPs from the same family — opened the fourth with a 45-yard pass to rookie tight end Kevin Boss. Five plays later, he hit Tyree on a 5-yard pass for a touchdown that gave the Giants an improbable 10-7 lead with 11:05 remaining.

Not surprisingly, Brady (29-for-48, 266 yards, one touchdown) answered back, riding receiver Wes Welker (11 catches, 103 yards) all the way down the field until he hit Randy Moss on a 6-yard touchdown pass with 2:42 remaining. All of a sudden, Brady had worked his magic and the Giants were down to their last chance.

The cool, calm, and always collected Manning said that's exactly where he wanted to be.

"You like being down four when you know you have to score a touchdown to win the Super Bowl," he said. "You can't write a better script. And to do it, it's just an unbelievable feeling."

Unbelievable, perhaps, but the Giants believed Manning would deliver. And to make sure they did, Strahan said that during the final drive he was walking up the sidelines telling his teammates: "The final score will be 17-14."

"I kept telling them, 'Repeat it,'" Strahan said. "I was walking up the sidelines saying, 'You say it. Repeat it. You have to believe it.' "

Manning made believers of everyone, especially

Giants defensive end Michael Strahan (92) celebrates after his sack of Tom Brady forced a fourth-and-13 for the Patriots during the third quarter. *Ron Antonelli/Daily News*

when he shocked his teammates by escaping the clutches of defensive end Jarvis Green and getting the ball in the perfect spot for Tyree to make what Tom Coughlin called "one of the all-time great plays in Super Bowl history."

Then it was up to the defense, which held New England to just 274 total yards, to stop the Patriots one more time.

When the Giants did, red white and blue confetti came shooting from everywhere, putting the final touches on what even Big Blue conceded was an improbable championship run.

"This team, this season, where we started, where we ended," Strahan said. "It's unexpected."

"The guys on this team and the run we've made, it's hard to believe," added Manning. "It really is."

And yet it's real. It happened. The Giants, who were once six inches away from an 0-3 start, are now the world champions. And they got there by beating the perfect — or near-perfect — team.

"Anytime you have a team that's 18-0 . . . stop and think about that," Coughlin said. "That's just an incredible accomplishment for them. But every team is beatable. You never know. The right moment, the right time . . . every team is beatable."

"We knew that if we played our best we'd have a chance to beat them," Manning added. "We believed the whole time."

The scrambling abilities of Giants quarterback Eli Manning were on display during the second half of the Super Bowl. *Corey Sipkin/Daily News*

SUPER BOWL

	1st	2nd	3rd	4th	Final
PATRIOTS	0	7	0	7	14
GIANTS	3	0	0	14	17

Scoring Summary

1st
GIANTS Lawrence Tynes, 32 yd field goal, 5:01. Drive: 16 plays, 63 yards in 9:59.
2nd
PATRIOTS Laurence Maroney, 1 yd run (Stephen Gostkowski kick is good), 14:57. Drive: 12 plays, 56 yards in 5:04.
4TH
GIANTS David Tyree, 5 yd pass from Eli Manning (Lawrence Tynes kick is good), 11:05. Drive: 6 plays, 80 yards in 3:47.
PATRIOTS Randy Moss, 6 yd pass from Tom Brady (Stephen Gostkowski kick is good), 2:42. Drive: 12 plays, 80 yards in 5:12.
GIANTS Plaxico Burress, 13 yd pass from Eli Manning (Lawrence Tynes kick is good), 0:35. Drive: 12 plays, 83 yards in 2:07.

Team Stats

	PATRIOTS	GIANTS
1st Downs	22	17
3rd-Down Conversions	7-14	8-16
4th-Down Conversions	0-2	1-1
Punts-Average	4-43.8	4-39.0
Punts-Returns	1-15	3-25
Kickoffs-Returns	4-94	2-39
Interceptions-Returns	1-23	0-0
Penalties-Yards	5-35	4-36
Fumbles-Lost	1-1	2-0
Time of Possession	29:33	30:27
Total Net Yards	274	338
Total Plays	69	63
Net Yards Rushing	45	91
Rushes	16	26
Net Yards Passing	229	247
Comp.-Att.-Int.	29-48-0	19-34-1
Sacked-Yards Lost	5-37	3-8
Red Zone Efficiency	2/2-100%	2/5-40%

Giants wide receiver Plaxico Burress catches a 13-yard pass in the end zone for the game-winning touchdown late in the fourth quarter. *Ron Antonelli/Daily News*

Giants head coach Tom Coughlin, arm raised, leads the celebration on field following New York's Super Bowl victory against New England. *Michael Appleton/Daily News*

GIANTS' VICTORY IS UPSET FOR THE AGES

February 5, 2008 ◆ By Hank Gola, Daily News

DYNASTIES DON'T LOSE Super Bowls, at least until Sunday night.

They might have eventually fallen off in any year and declined, but when dynasty teams reached the biggest stage in the past, they always won.

The Packers of the '60s won theirs. The Steelers of the '70s won theirs. The 49ers of the '80s and '90s won theirs and so did the Cowboys of the '90s. Usually big.

The Patriots of this decade were supposed to surpass all those with the single greatest season of all time for a fourth championship in seven years. By knocking them off their immortal perch, the wild-card Giants manufactured one of the greatest upsets in history.

But was it the greatest? Was it greater than the AFL Jets' epic win over the NFL Colts' in Super Bowl III? Greater than the Patriots' dismantling of the Rams' Greatest Show on Turf in Super Bowl XXXVI? Greater than the granddaddy of all upsets, the Sneakers Game, when the 1934 Giants, an 8-5 outfit, beat the 13-0 Bears?

Let's put that one aside because the frozen field had so much to do with it. Most people will still point to Joe Namath's guaranteed win as the gold standard because of its ramifications. It wasn't just about the supposed disparity between two teams. It was about two leagues. There were so few football writers who picked the Jets to win the game that

their names actually hang in the Hall of Fame in Canton along with their predictions.

The Chiefs and Raiders were no match for the mighty Packers in the first two Super Bowls and the Jets, cocky as they were, were supposed to be mere fodder for the Colts. The Jets' 16-7 victory forever changed the perception of the two leagues and ushered in a new era for professional football.

Or did it?

You could argue the only reason the Jets were such heavy underdogs was because of the arrogance of the old guard NFL and its supporters. Match up the talent on the teams now and it doesn't seem that one-sided at all. And while the soon-to-be-swallowed-up AFL was in euphoria over the Jets' win, it took another year before people were convinced of the parity between the leagues. Even after the Jets' win, the Chiefs were still a big underdog before they took apart the Vikings in Super Bowl IV, the last before the merger.

As for Super Bowl XXXVI, the Patriots were 14-point underdogs but looking back, is anyone still surprised they pulled it off with what they would do over the next several years? As explosive as those Rams were, match up that talent in hindsight and rethink the point spread. That was more a changing of the guard as dominance continued to swing toward the AFC, a dominance that was still in effect, it seemed, as the 2007 season played itself

Giants defensive end Michael Strahan goes airborne as he applies pressure to Patriots quarterback Tom Brady. *Michael Appleton/Daily News*

out.

At one point, the Patriots and Colts were supposed to be on their own level, followed by the Cowboys and maybe the Packers. The Giants weren't even in the discussion. They were a third-tier team, at best, a playoff contender, maybe, but not much more.

Put it into context and the Giants' heist of the Vince Lombardi Trophy has to be considered the greatest upset run of all time. Against the Bucs, they were three-point underdogs against a play-off nemesis in Jeff Garcia. Against the Cowboys, they were the first NFC team since 1987 to knock off the top-seeded team in the divisional round. Against the Packers, they outplayed Green Bay in its own frigid elements. Finally, they completed the journey by mauling the Patriots.

It's true, unlike Super Bowl III, there were many experts who gave the Giants a chance because they had the elements to give the Patriots problems, as seen in Week 17. But while

New England was seen as a more vulnerable team down the stretch, the shock value can't be dismissed, because, in reality, the Giants dominated this game.

Had the Patriots made Brady's fourth-quarter drive stand up, the game still would have been a textbook example of how a team can impose its physical presence on the other. And did anyone ever think Bill Belichick could be so badly outcoached?

As Michael Strahan said, the Giants not only shocked the world, they shocked themselves.

"We did it to prove to ourselves that we can defy all the odds," Strahan said. "To all the people who picked the Patriots, you'd be a fool not to pick the Patriots. They had every weapon, they were destined to win and I don't blame you."

Biggest upset ever? You be the judge.

A deep pass to Giants receiver Steve Smith in the end zone goes incomplete to finish play in the first half. *Michael Appleton/Daily News*

At a celebration held at the Meadowlands on Feb. 5, 2008, David Tyree mimicks his Super Bowl catch that kept alive the team's fourth-quarter, game-winning drive. *Andrew Theodorakis/Daily News*

REPEAT ALREADY HAS NICE RING TO CHAMPION GIANTS

February 5, 2008 • By Ralph Vacchiano, Daily News

THE RED, WHITE and blue confetti was still swirling around the stadium, and most of the newly crowned champions were still in their pads when Michael Strahan told the world this was only the beginning. The Giants, he said, "were trying to start their own dynasty."

In other words, winning a Super Bowl championship was nice. But what they really want is to do it again.

"That's what you want to do," Giants GM Jerry Reese said Monday, as the Super Bowl champs began checking out of their team hotel. "You want to get to this game and you want to win it, but we have a really young team. We just don't want to go away. Hopefully we can stay on top and not have a Super Bowl and then just disappear."

It's a bold goal, since only three teams in the last 14 years have managed to even reach consecutive Super Bowls, but it was a goal the Giants set almost immediately after they knocked off the previously unbeaten Patriots, 17-14, in Super Bowl XLII. Justin Tuck talked of how he and Michael Strahan discussed repeating during their postgame shower. And it was brought up several times yesterday morning by bleary-eyed players who partied all night and hardly slept at all.

"Just because you have success and you win a championship doesn't mean you stop for a year, or you become content with what you've done," said Eli Manning, the Super Bowl MVP. "If anything, I think it should make you strive even harder to try and get here again. You've had this feeling, you've had this taste and you don't want it to leave.

"But we're going to have to work even harder and better, and that's our goal, to become a better team. Once we get back to working in March or April, it's going to be about, 'What can you do this year?' Last year is behind you, and we've celebrated for that month or two that you have off, and now it's back to work to see if you can do it again."

One reason there have only been two repeat champions in the last 14 years is because it's easy to lose that competitive drive or edge when your dreams have already come true. That could be especially difficult for a Giants team that played with a chip on its shoulder all season. It's hard to

> "YOU'VE HAD THIS FEELING, YOU'VE HAD THIS TASTE AND YOU DON'T WANT IT TO LEAVE."
> —ELI MANNING

play the "no respect" angle when you're carrying the Lombardi Trophy.

Then again, the Giants were master motivators for themselves all season. So it's certainly worth a try.

"We still feel a little bit of a sense of people saying that the Patriots lost," defensive tackle Barry Cofield said. "They're saying, 'The Patriots didn't do this. The Patriots didn't do that.' They're disappointed. But I don't think it's about them. It should be about us. We still feel like a poor man's champ."

Maybe that's because the reality of it all hadn't quite sunk in yesterday morning. The players were wandering about the hotel with their families and friends, signing autographs, hugging everyone, and wearing their Super Bowl championship hats. They were dreaming of today's ticker-tape parade and subsequent celebration at Giants Stadium.

It still didn't feel quite real.

"It's all surreal," Tuck said. "It's kind of like I'm dreaming right now. I'm not normally at a loss for words, but right now I really am. I've never experienced anything like this."

Now, of course, he wants to experience it again — something no Giants team has ever done. In fact, only the Denver Broncos (XXXII and XXXII) and the New England Patriots (XXXVIII and XXXIX) have repeated as champions in the last 14 seasons. The Patriots, of course, have been to four Super Bowls (winning three) in the last seven years.

"New England, they kind of set the bar high," Reese said. "The league's not built for a team to stay on top like they have for so long, but that's what we want to do. We want to be able to stay on top and follow that pattern."

"We'll get back to work and we're going to be hungry," added guard Rich Seubert. "And we're going to want to do it again."

Giants head coach Tom Coughlin shows off the Super Bowl trophy to fans at a celebration at the Meadowlands on Feb. 5, 2008. *Kevin Hagen/Daily News*

REGULAR SEASON TEAM STATS

	Giants	Opponents
TOTAL FIRST DOWNS	321	288
FIRST DOWNS (Rushing-Passing-By Penalty)	119-167-35	83-185-20
THIRD DOWN CONVERSIONS	91/219	73/211
FOURTH DOWN CONVERSIONS	6/17	10/16
TOTAL OFFENSIVE YARDS	5,302	4,880
OFFENSE (Plays-Average Yards)	1,041-5.1	984-5.0
TOTAL RUSHING YARDS	2,148	1,563
RUSHING (Plays-Average Yards)	469-4.6	408-3.8
TOTAL PASSING YARDS	3,154	3,317
PASSING (Comp-Att-Int-Avg)	302-544-20-6.2	306-523-15-7.0
SACKS	53	28
FIELD GOALS	23/27	21/29
TOUCHDOWNS	44	41
TDs (Rushing-Passing-Returns-Defensive)	15-23-1-5	12-24-1-4
TIME OF POSSESSION	31:21	28:38

REGULAR SEASON INDIVIDUAL STATS

PASSING

Player	Att	Comp	Yards	Comp%	Yards/Att	TD	INT	Sack	Rating
Eli Manning	529	297	3,336	56.1	6.3	23	20	27	73.9
Jared Lorenzen	8	4	28	50.0	3.5	0	0	1	58.3
Anthony Wright	7	1	12	14.3	1.7	0	0	0	39.6

RUSHING

Player	Att	Yards	Yards/Att	Long	TD
Brandon Jacobs	202	1,009	5.0	43	4
Derrick Ward	125	602	4.8	44	3
Reuben Droughns	85	275	3.2	45	6
Eli Manning	29	69	2.4	18	1
Ahmad Bradshaw	23	190	8.3	88	1
Jeremy Shockey	1	6	6.0	6	0
Sinorice Moss	1	4	4.0	4	0
Jared Lorenzen	1	2	2.0	2	0
Anthony Wright	1	-1	-1.0	-1	0
Domenik Hixon	1	-8	-8.0	-8	0

RECEIVING

Player	Rec	Yards	Yards/Rec	Long	TD
Plaxico Burress	70	1,025	14.6	60	12
Amani Toomer	59	760	12.9	40	3
Jeremy Shockey	57	619	10.9	29	3
Derrick Ward	26	179	6.9	17	1
Brandon Jacobs	23	174	7.6	34	2
Sinorice Moss	21	225	10.7	20	0
Kevin Boss	9	118	13.1	23	2
Steve Smith	8	63	7.9	12	0
Reuben Droughns	7	49	7.0	11	0
Madison Hedgecock	6	45	7.5	9	0
Michael Matthews	6	28	4.7	6	0
David Tyree	4	35	8.8	24	0
Ahmad Bradshaw	2	12	6.0	11	0
Domenik Hixon	1	5	5.0	5	0

FIELD GOALS

Player	1-19	20-29	30-39	40-49	50+
Lawrence Tynes	1/1	9/10	5/8	8/8	0/0

PUNTING

Player	Punts	Avg	Touchbacks	Inside 20	Long	Block
Jeff Feagles	71	40.4	5	25	60	1

PUNT RETURNS

Player	Returns	FC	Yards/Ret	Long	TD
R.W. McQuarters	42	18	7.6	27	0
Ahmad Bradshaw	1	0	1.0	1	0

KICKOFF RETURNS

Player	Returns	Yards	Yards/Ret	Long	TD
Ahmad Bradshaw	38	921	24.2	68	0
Reuben Droughns	20	437	21.9	34	0
Domenik Hixon	8	221	27.6	74	1

DEFENSE

Player	Tackles	Solo	Assist	Sacks	Fumble Rec
Gibril Wilson	92	78	14	0	0
Antonio Pierce	103	77	26	1	1
Sam Madison	67	59	8	1	1
Kawika Mitchell	76	54	22	4	2
Justin Tuck	65	48	17	10	2
James Butler	61	45	16	0	0
Michael Strahan	57	45	12	9	1
Osi Umenyiora	52	40	12	13	5
Aaron Ross	42	35	7	2	0
Mathias Kiwanuka	46	34	12	4	0
Kevin Dockery	46	31	15	0	1
Fred Robbins	42	31	11	6	0
Barry Cofield	34	29	5	1	0
Reggie Torbor	39	27	12	1	0
Michael Johnson	25	23	2	0	1
Chase Blackburn	22	20	2	0	0
Corey Webster	18	17	1	0	0
Craig Dahl	19	16	3	0	0
R.W. McQuarters	15	14	1	0	0
Gerris Wilkinson	14	10	4	0	0
Ahmad Bradshaw	9	9	0	0	1
Domenik Hixon	11	8	3	0	0
David Tyree	9	7	2	0	0
Zak DeOssie	6	6	0	0	0
Reuben Droughns	7	5	2	0	1
David Diehl	4	4	0	0	0
Rich Seubert	3	3	0	0	0
Jeremy Shockey	3	3	0	0	0
Russell Davis	5	2	3	0	0
Dave Tollefson	4	2	2	0	0
Eli Manning	2	2	0	0	0
Lawrence Tynes	2	2	0	0	0
Derrick Ward	2	2	0	0	0
Michael Matthews	2	2	0	0	0
Amani Toomer	2	2	0	0	0
Madison Hedgecock	2	1	1	0	0
Manuel Wright	2	1	1	0	0
Danny Ware	1	1	0	0	0
Chris Snee	1	1	0	0	0
Grey Ruegamer	1	1	0	0	0
Shaun O'Hara	1	1	0	0	0
Kareem McKenzie	1	1	0	0	0
Kevin Boss	1	1	0	0	0
Plaxico Burress	1	1	0	0	0
Jay Alford	1	1	0	1	0
Torrance Daniels	1	0	1	0	0
Patrick Pass	1	0	1	0	0

INTERCEPTIONS

Player	Int	Yards	Yards/Int	Long	TD
Sam Madison	4	59	14.8	27	0
Gibril Wilson	4	12	3.0	10	0
Aaron Ross	3	51	17.0	43	1
Corey Webster	1	34	34.0	34	1
Antonio Pierce	1	28	28.0	28	0
Kawika Mitchell	1	20	20.0	20	1
James Butler	1	0	0.0	0	0

POSTSEASON TEAM STATS

	Giants	Opponents
TOTAL FIRST DOWNS	73	78
FIRST DOWNS (Rushing-Passing-By Penalty)	21-46-6	21-49-8
THIRD DOWN CONVERSIONS	23/53	27/54
FOURTH DOWN CONVERSIONS	1/2	0/3
TOTAL OFFENSIVE YARDS	1,222	1,145
OFFENSE (Plays-Average Yards)	246-5.0	251-4.6
TOTAL RUSHING YARDS	415	296
RUSHING (Plays-Average Yards)	118-3.5	85-3.5
TOTAL PASSING YARDS	807	849
PASSING (Comp-Att-Int-Avg)	72-119-1-7.2	89-158-5-5.8
SACKS	8	9
FIELD GOALS	5/7	3/3
TOUCHDOWNS	10	8
TDs (Rushing-Passing-Returns-Defensive)	4-6-0-0	3-5-0-0
TIME OF POSSESSION	31:52	28:46

Giants offensive lineman Guy Whimper (left) and defensive end Justin Tuck reach out to the crowd lining the street during the team's victory parade on Feb. 5, 2008. *Craig Warga/Daily News*

The Daily News acknowledges the following individuals for their contributions to this book and coverage of the Giants' championship season. Space limitations preclude us from naming all the writers, photographers, editors and designers who made the Daily News' Giants coverage the best in New York City, but the contents of this book would not have been possible without the hard work of:

Jim Rich, Deputy Sports Editor
Teri Thompson, Sunday Sports Editor
Eric Barrow, Deputy Sunday Sports Editor
Bill Price, Deputy Sports Editor, Nights
Angela Trosi, Photo Sales Editor
Samantha Yee, Sales Assistant

Daily News NFL writers: Ralph Vacchiano, Gary Myers, Mike Lupica, Rich Cimini, Hank Gola, Ohm Youngmisuk, Filip Bondy, Tim Smith, Ian Begley and Vic Ziegel

Daily News photographers: Linda Cataffo, Michael Appleton, Corey Sipkin, Lee Weissman, Ron Antonelli, Robert Sabo, Kevin Hagen and Andrew Theodorakis